Psychic Reiki

Unlock the Secrets of Psychic Development and Energy Healing Using Your Hands

© Copyright 2022 - All rights reserved.

The content contained within this book may not be reproduced, duplicated, or transmitted without direct written permission from the author or the publisher.

Under no circumstances will any blame or legal responsibility be held against the publisher, or author, for any damages, reparation, or monetary loss due to the information contained within this book, either directly or indirectly.

Legal Notice:

This book is copyright protected. It is only for personal use. You cannot amend, distribute, sell, use, quote, or paraphrase any part, or the content within this book, without the consent of the author or publisher.

Disclaimer Notice:

Please note the information contained within this document is for educational and entertainment purposes only. All effort has been executed to present accurate, up-to-date, reliable, and complete information. No warranties of any kind are declared or implied. Readers acknowledge that the author is not engaging in the rendering of legal, financial, medical, or professional advice. The content within this book has been derived from various sources. Please consult a licensed professional before attempting any techniques outlined in this book.

By reading this document, the reader agrees that under no circumstances is the author responsible for any losses, direct or indirect, that are incurred as a result of the use of the information contained within this document, including, but not limited to, errors, omissions, or inaccuracies.

Your Free Gift (only available for a limited time)

Thanks for getting this book! If you want to learn more about various spirituality topics, then join Mari Silva's community and get a free guided meditation MP3 for awakening your third eye. This guided meditation mp3 is designed to open and strengthen ones third eye so you can experience a higher state of consciousness. Simply visit the link below the image to get started.

https://spiritualityspot.com/meditation

Table of Contents

INTRODUCTION 1
CHAPTER 1: PSYCHIC REIKI EXPLAINED 3
CHAPTER 2: ENERGY AND CHAKRAS 12
CHAPTER 3: MEDITATION AND VISUALIZATION 29
CHAPTER 4: WORKING WITH YOUR GUIDES 39
CHAPTER 5: CLEARING AND GROUNDING 49
CHAPTER 6: DEVELOPING YOUR PSYCHIC ABILITIES 57
CHAPTER 7: PSYCHIC REIKI PRACTICUM 1 - HEALING YOURSELF 66
CHAPTER 8: PSYCHIC REIKI PRACTICUM 2 - HEALING OTHERS 78
CHAPTER 9: PSYCHIC REIKI PRACTICUM 3 - PSYCHIC DISTANCE HEALING 88
CHAPTER 10: ACTIVATE YOUR THIRD EYE TEMPLE 96
CHAPTER 11: THE PSYCHIC REIKI TOOLKIT: CRYSTALS, TALISMANS, TRINKETS, AND TAROT 104
CONCLUSION 111
HERE'S ANOTHER BOOK BY MARI SILVA THAT YOU MIGHT LIKE 113
YOUR FREE GIFT (ONLY AVAILABLE FOR A LIMITED TIME) 114
REFERENCES 115

Introduction

Many alternative medicine and energy healing therapy forms have gained popularity in the last few years. Yoga, meditation, herbal medicine, and Reiki have proven to be effective methods for helping millions of people in the US and around the world heal and become healthier. Consequently, more people want to learn about this fascinating subject out of curiosity or because they hope to become Reiki practitioners.

If you are a psychic familiar with Reiki and hoping to mix the two together and expand your knowledge, then this book is for you. We understand that these topics can be complicated, especially for beginners, so we have made sure that we straightforwardly present them so that both beginners and advanced learners can understand and relate to the material.

Beginners will find all the information they need to start their psychic Reiki journey. You will find the topic presented in detail using simple terminologies to avoid confusing or overwhelming the reader. We will also discuss related topics like energy, chakras, meditation, and visualization to help you be better equipped and informed as a practitioner.

We want this book to serve as a guide to which you can return whenever you have any questions about energy or Reiki or looking for guidance. For this reason, you'll find various instructions and hands-on methods you can use while healing yourself or others. A practitioner specializing in psychic Reiki needs tools like tarots and crystals to help them access healing energy. However, some new practitioners may be unfamiliar with the necessary items required during a healing session. In this book, you'll find all the information you need about the tools practitioners use during Reiki practice.

You will find all the answers for Reiki, healing, and developing psychic abilities. We have done extensive research to provide accurate information to help you start your career or satisfy your curiosity. Learning a new subject can be challenging. There is always confusion; the more you learn, the more questions you have. However, if your source material provides clear and detailed information, you'll have more answers than questions and build a strong foundation. This is precisely why we have made that we have covered every angle so you would feel a sense of satisfaction and accomplishment after reading this book and be prepared to advance and reach an expert level.

Being a psychic is a gift, a rare ability only a few have. If you are one of these lucky people, take advantage of your unique abilities to heal yourself and others. Let this book be your guide to take the world of psychic Reiki by storm. There is not a more noble cause than helping people. Diseases require doctors, but ailments of the soul will require someone like you with a healing touch. Understanding Reiki and using your psychic abilities can help others feel better and encourage healing.

This book will put you on the first steps on your journey as a psychic Reiki practitioner and a healer. So, let us take this journey together and heal.

Chapter 1: Psychic Reiki Explained

Today, more people are looking for alternative therapies to complement their allopathic treatments for their illnesses. People worldwide are exploring options such as healing crystals, cupping, acupressure, acupuncture, and Reiki.

The last of those, Reiki, is the one that tends to cause the most confusion in people. Many have never heard of this practice, and those who have heard of it often do not understand it properly, leading to them dismissing it as another fraud or fad. However, once you understand the techniques that comprise Reiki (and psychic Reiki), you'll soon understand that it has quite a bit of validity.

This book will take you through the basics of Reiki and will also help you explore psychic Reiki in particular in further detail. When you turn the final page, you'll truly understand why so many people recommend psychic Reiki as a healing technique.

What Is Reiki?

Originating in Japan, Reiki is an energy healing technique based on the belief that vital energy flows through each person's body. The practice helps to relax the body and remove stress.

The simplest way to describe it is that Reiki is performed through a series of gentle touches. Practitioners essentially use their hands to provide your body with energy and do so in a way focused on improving the flow and balance of your body's natural stores of vital energy.

The "patient" generally sits on a massage table during a Reiki session. You will either be fully clothed or covered with sheets or a blanket during this process, and your Reiki practitioner will gently lay their hands on your body or allow them to hover over it. The parts of your body over which the practitioners lay their hands are those where the flow of vital energy is especially potent.

A practitioner will cover your major organs, chakras, and major meridians with their hands, transferring energy as needed. Many patients have found that, during this process, they unwittingly fall into a trance-like state where they experience incredibly vivid and lucid dreams. This experience is so common that it has a name, the "Reiki sleep."

Reiki practitioners often dislike being called healers. They believe that their job is to provide a patient's body with the energy it needs to complete the necessary healing on its own. According to them, people frequently run around low or empty on energy in the modern world. A person's natural energy store is generally expended on their daily activities, such as work and travel.

This means that your body has no extra energy left over to focus on healing, especially healing more than just superficially. That is where Reiki practitioners come in, and they provide your body with the additional energy needed to heal itself.

Reiki is a combination of two words. In the Japanese language, "Red" is translated as "high power," and "ki" is life energy, not just in us but in everything. The name tells new adherents exactly what this practice offers, focusing on the universal, or spiritual, life force energy we all have.

The History of Reiki

Mikao Usui founded the practice of Reiki. Born to a Japanese Buddhist family in 1865, Usui was raised as a samurai and was trained in swordsmanship, martial arts, specifically the Japanese techniques of Aiki, and other similar disciplines. As an adult, he developed an interest in medicine, psychology, and theology and traveled around the world (including the United States) to continue his studies in these topics.

By the early 1920s, he had joined a Buddhist monastery as a priest and monk. As part of his time in the monastery, he spent 21 days on Mount Kurama praying and fasting. It is believed that during these 21 days, Usui was shown the Sanskrit symbols that would help him develop his system of Reiki.

Usui set up his first Reiki school and clinic in Tokyo in 1922, teaching students the art and encouraging them to spread the practice worldwide. One of his best-known students was Chujiro Hayashi, a former naval surgeon who was instrumental in spreading Reiki outside Japan, especially to the United States, through his student Hawayo Takata.

Hawayo Takata was a Japanese-American woman who initially approached Hayashi for healing in the 1930s. After being healed, she stayed on to learn Reiki under Hayashi, eventually becoming a Reiki master. Believing Reiki had immense value, Takata decided to bring the practice with her back to the United States.

However, as Reiki was a Japanese practice, she was also aware of the challenges that could arise from possible resistance by the public, and the political situation between the US and Japan was sensitive. She had returned to the United States in the 1940s, right before the Second World War, when international tensions were high. This issue would persist following the war's end, especially as the United States and Japan were on opposite sides of the war.

Believing that Reiki's value to the world could not be ignored, she chose to alter the history of Reiki's development and Mikao Usui's life to make it more appealing to the West. She claimed that, rather than a Buddhist with a background in the samurai tradition, Usui was actually a dean of a Christian school in Japan.

Additionally, Usui had developed many of his Reiki principles through studying the Buddhist religious book "Tantra of the Lightning Flash." To make it more in line with the beliefs of Western audiences, she claimed that he had instead been inspired by the story of Jesus Christ, who was able to heal with the touch of a hand and had traveled to the US and other Western countries in an attempt to learn more about Reiki.

Hawayo Takata was successful in her work and managed to help spread Reiki around the United States and, eventually, the world. She trained several Reiki masters herself, who further helped grow the discipline.

Aside from Takata, the only other student trained by Hayashi who practiced and taught Reiki in public was Chiyoko Yamaguchi. Yamaguchi continued to work in Japan, and while Takata had to alter her practice of Reiki to allow for internationalization, Yamaguchi continued to practice Reiki exactly as taught to her by Hayashi. In 1999, she founded the Jikiden Reiki Institute in Tokyo, where Reiki is taught the same way Hayashi taught her in the 1930s.

Principles of Reiki

Five main Reiki principles may sound similar to other affirmations you may incorporate into your daily life. Let us look at them in further detail:

Just for today, I release angry thoughts.

According to Reiki, the anger you feel at events such as dealing with someone rude to you comes from the anger energy already within you. This Reiki principle calls on you to release that energy by recognizing the anger in your life and letting it go. This, in turn, allows you to replace that anger with happiness.

Just for today, I'm grateful.

This is a reminder to be grateful for all the small moments in your life, moments that you would otherwise watch rush by without thinking twice. If you focus on what is beneficial in your life, you attract positive healing toward you.

Just for today, I release thoughts of worry.

Worry is ever-present in most of our lives. Worry about things that are happening, things that haven't yet happened, and things that may or may not happen. Like anger, Reiki holds that worry comes from within, and this principle invites people to release that worry energy so that they can live easier in the present.

Just for today, I'm gentle with all beings.

This principle is a reminder to be kind and compassionate to all people and beings around you and to consider looking at alternative perspectives to see the world from other beings' eyes. At the same time, it is a reminder to be gentle, kind, and compassionate with yourself because you are encompassed within the phrase "all beings."

Just for today, I expand my consciousness.

Recognize who you are and how you fit into this world as an individual and part of a larger ecosystem. Focus on how you live your life and how that affects everyone around you.

Aside from these five Reiki principles, a few variations are sometimes considered in place of one or more of the above principles. These are:

Just for today, I am humble.

This Reiki principle reminds us that, while our egos would like nothing more than to brag and show off about our accomplishments, we must consider taking things down a notch. Instead, take the chance to bow down, learn from others, and enjoy loving and being loved in return.

Just for today, I am honest/Just for today, I will learn my living honestly.

Though these principles sound relatively similar, they can actually be quite different in practice.

The first, "Just for today, I am honest," reminds you to be your most authentic self as much as possible instead of trying to fit into a pre-destined mold. It is a reminder to let your real self shine and, if necessary, to do so in baby steps, starting with doing so for a single day ("just for today") and then going from there.

The second, "Just for today, I will learn my living honestly," is a reminder to live honestly, without relying on lying, cheating, or otherwise harming others to get ahead. It is a reminder that while money can make life materially easy, it is not and should not be the measure of how successful you are. Instead, you should strive for abundance in all areas of your life, rather than just monetarily.

Just for today, I will honor my parents, teachers, and elders.

This principle is a reminder to celebrate your roots and those who have helped guide you to where you are currently. This does not mean idealizing them or placing them on a pedestal, but rather acknowledging their very real contributions and learning and growing yourself as a person thanks to the lessons they have taught and will teach you.

Reiki Symbols and Attunements

Reiki symbols allow you to use the energy of your Reiki practice for a specific purpose rather than leaving it directionless. They help change how Reiki functions generate energy. They can be activated by visualizing them, speaking their names verbally, or drawing them. The most important part of the activation process is the intention rather than how the symbols are thought of.

You will learn more about the Reiki symbols and how to use them in later chapters, so keep reading to learn more!

Reiki attunement is a process the Reiki master goes through during a class with a student. This helps open up the student's energy system, helping them connect to the universal Reiki energy and become a vessel for that energy to use to heal themselves and others.

The energy pathways are opened through a series of symbols, allowing energy to flow freely through the student's body. Some students report that this process enhances other channeling and healing pathways in the body, with reports of increased intuitive awareness and psychic sensitivity.

Psychic Reiki

So, you are already well-versed in Reiki, but the title of this book is "psychic Reiki" rather than simply Reiki.

So, what is psychic Reiki? Why does "psychic" have anything to do with Reiki?

In the simplest of terms, psychic Reiki is an energy healing modality in which the practitioner's psychic abilities are utilized for healing purposes. You do not need special symbols or movements.

Instead, you'll use intuition to direct your energy from your body to someone else's.

In other words, think of psychic Reiki as telepathic Reiki or even intuitive Reiki. It has the same benefits of "regular" Reiki practice but is done without the focus on the practitioner's/Reiki master's physical body it involves. Thus, one can do away with the traditional symbols and hand positions and instead fully trust the Reiki master's innate abilities.

Psychic Reiki is particularly powerful for individuals who are hesitant to be touched by others for many reasons, including PTSD and past trauma.

How to Check if You Are Psychic and Will Be Good at Healing

Are you hoping to get into practicing psychic Reiki? If so, here is a checklist that you can refer to determine whether or not you have psychic abilities:

- Lucid dreaming
- Precognitive dreams or visions
- Awareness or knowledge of people, places, and things that have no rational explanation and are not explained by events in your personal history that you may have consciously forgotten
- Having a remembrance or recognition of your or others' past lives.
- Hearing voices that are not your own or those of others in the room with you or in hearing distance of you
- Having a "built-in" ability to tell the truth from a lie and other such gut feelings.
- Feeling emotions out of nowhere that seem relatively nonsensical until an event happens soon after that explains it, such as a family member calling with good news after a moment of delight, or a friend receiving bad news after you felt down in the dumps all of a sudden
- Experiencing déjà vu frequently and often

- Having people with psychic powers in the family
- Hypersensitivity to negativity, noise, and other people's emotions
- Very sharp senses. One enhanced sense is the most common, though multiple are possible.
- Recurring dreams that you are unable to explain

If you can check off one-third or more of the above list, it is a good indication that you have some form of psychic abilities.

You can also check to determine if you have healing powers. Here is a checklist to ponder:

- You feel most at home in nature
- You are very sensitive
- You feel a calling that draws you to look for ways to heal or ease the suffering of other beings
- You have especially vivid dreams
- You are very creative
- You are very intuitive
- You are an empath
- You can often feel tingling in your hands and palms. This is a sign that energy is collecting in these areas, looking for a way out through healing others
- You have already had to heal yourself or have suffered a life-threatening or chronic illness yourself
- You are a natural peacemaker when working with two people feuding with each other
- You are a natural loner, introvert, or get overwhelmed in public easily
- You have a history of healers in your family. These can be spiritual healers with healing powers or more "traditional" healers like doctors and nurses as well
- You are a good listener
- You can feel the energy within yourself. More than that, you can also distinguish between different types of energy within yourself and alter it if needed

- You have undergone several mystical experiences

If you can relate to one-third or more of the above checklist, it is a good sign that you have healing powers and/or intentions.

This book will cover everything you need to know about honing your psychic and healing powers through psychic Reiki. In the next few chapters, we will walk you through the life force energy you'll be working with and the seven primary chakras. We will also walk you through meditation and visualization, including the hand positions as recommended by Mikao Usui's Gassho Kokyo-ho meditation technique.

We will also explore how you can work with your Spirit Guides and what clearing and grounding are. We will cover why clearing and grounding are important before any form of healing.

We will then help you develop your psychic abilities further. These abilities are often known as the "Clairs," and this book will ensure that you can use them effectively in your practice of psychic Reiki. Then, we will move on to three psychic Reiki practicums so you can use the knowledge you have gained practically and effectively.

Finally, we will also help you explore how you can activate your Third Eye Temple, which can, in turn, further enhance your psychic practice. We will also provide you with a psychic Reiki "toolkit," the tools you can use to complement your psychic reiki practice, such as crystals, tarot, talismans, Reiki water, and more.

If psychic Reiki sounds like something you want to explore further, you are in the right place. All that is left for you to do is turn to the next page!

Chapter 2: Energy and Chakras

Can a chef learn how to cook without any knowledge of food? The same principle applies to energy healers. Before becoming a Reiki practitioner, you should first know what energy is. Why is it important? What is life force energy? Answering these questions will prepare you as you begin your journey to become a psychic Reiki practitioner.

What Is Lifeforce Energy?

Lifeforce energy is a concept that exists in various cultures worldwide and goes by many names, such as prana, Qi, Holy Spirit, ki, anima, inner wind, ruh, and pneuma. It goes back to our ancient ancestors who understood the importance of energy and its role in our lives. They regarded energy as a source you can use for healing and developed many practices around this concept. Life force is a cosmic energy that exists everywhere around us. As it enters our brains, this energy acts like a phone charger that charges our cells and brings them back to life. Everything in the universe has life force energy flowing through them, humans, animals, plants, water, crystals, and even the Earth. Vital for our survival, this energy acts like a heartbeat, indicating whether we are alive or not.

However, energy can be drained one way or another. For this reason, we need life force energy to sustain us. Acting as the foundation of our being, this subtle energy is responsible for every action we take; it defines who we are. It is responsible for all of our body's functions like breathing, blood flow, digestion, and even our body's movements. Life force energy provides us with consciousness and awareness to experience life; without it, we cease to exist.

Life force energy has been mentioned in various ancient texts, which means the concept has been around for thousands of years. Energy is not a modern idea. The world we know today came to be due to an energy explosion known as the Big Bang Theory. Ever since energy has flowed through everything and everyone, this provides an interesting perspective to view the world around you. Everything on Earth came from the same energy, which connects us all by the energy that brought us here.

The Chinese referred to life force energy as "Qi." If you are familiar with traditional Chinese medicine, you may like to know that it is based around Qi which mainly focuses on the energy flow inside our bodies.

We are not just physical bodies; we are much more. We are our thoughts, feelings, and spirit, all of which are connected to the life force in one way or another. Our energies can affect our physical health, mental health, and well-being. Doctors rarely pay attention to ailments that are caused by disrupted energy. So, what do we do when our energy needs tending? We seek the help of a Reiki practitioner. Plenty of alternative medicine like acupuncture revolves around Qi energy and has been adapted to western medicine. Practitioners that work with Qi can recognize the energy in their patient's aura and manipulate it to detect diseases.

The Hindus referred to the life force as "Prana." It is a Sanskrit word that means "breath." Prana first appeared in Sanskrit texts like the Vedas 3000 years ago. In various Hindu literature texts, the sun was described as the source of prana, connecting the four elements, earth, air, water, and fire. Prana, just like its Chinese counterpart, Qi, has a huge impact on our health and is responsible for various bodily functions like breathing and digestion. According to ancient texts, we have various channels in our bodies through which prana flows. These channels are called nadis, and we have about 72,000 of them in our bodies. Nadis are quite similar to the modern description of the nervous system and nerves. Although thousands of Nadis are in our bodies, you'll find three main ones that are always referenced: Sushumna, Ida, and Lingala. These three main Nadis travel from the base of the spine up to the head.

Our senses depend on our life force to flow, which is what heals. We use our senses, and the healing comes from inside, aided by our nervous system, which distributes that energy.

The Subtle Bodies

More often than not, when people discuss bodies, they mean the physical body, which is the most popular concept. However, there is always more to us humans than what meets the eyes. Although we can not see them or touch them, each person has seven subtle bodies, and each one vibrates at a different frequency. These subtle bodies are energy layers connected and encompass the aura. They interact with the physical and non-physical worlds using energy.

According to the ancient Hindu text Bhagavad Gita, the subtle body governs over the physical body and consists of the ego, mind, and intellect. The seven subtle bodies can be divided into physical, spiritual, and astral. There are three bodies in the physical, and they are responsible for the physical plane's energy. Three in the spiritual and are responsible for the spiritual realm, while the astral body is what connects these bodies together. The subtle spiritual bodies are known to vibrate at a higher frequency than the physical ones.

Subtle bodies are not a new concept. In fact, they were mentioned in various ancient cultures like Native America, Ancient Egypt, Chinese, and Ancient India (Sanskrit).

Becoming a psychic Reiki practitioner requires working with energy and learning to manipulate it. You should become familiar with the seven subtle bodies to navigate the spiritual world.

The Etheric Body

Of all the seven subtle bodies, the etheric body is considered the closest to the physical body, located just a couple of inches from it. This subtle body transforms the universe's energy to supply the physical body with what it needs to survive and function properly. As a result of this proximity, the etheric body has a huge impact on our bodily functions.

The etheric body is the densest of all the subtle bodies. For this reason, and since it is the closest to the physical body, it has the lowest frequency. Reiki practitioners should pay close attention to the etheric body because it is directly impacted by various alternative healing methods like acupuncture, Qigong, and Reiki.

The Emotional Body

As the name implies, the emotional body is responsible for our feelings and emotions. Located three inches from the physical body, the emotional body can impact our physical and mental health and our souls because our emotions can affect different areas of our lives. The emotional body's aura is the only one that changes colors and shape depending on a person's mood. For instance, if you are angry, depressed, anxious, or in love, the color and shape of your aura change every time. Once you learn how to read people's auras, you'll be able to determine their moods from their aura's color.

The Mental Body

This subtle body is located a little further from the previously mentioned subtle bodies. Located three to eight inches away from the physical body, the mental body is responsible for our memory, thoughts, imagination, intuition, creativity, logic, and how we gather and process information. It directly impacts the mind, and when it is not functioning properly, it can affect our creativity and concentration. Since our minds never stop working and are always racing with thoughts, the mental body is always glowing in the color yellow.

However, on some occasions, when the mind shuts down, such as when we sleep or after meditation, this subtle body becomes discolored—it can switch color based on our emotions and thoughts. For instance, if you think about how much you miss someone and you get sad, the color of the emotional body aura will change. This affects our mood, and the body's aura will change to mirror that.

The Astral Body

The astral body is perfectly positioned to create a connection between the spirit real and our physical body. Through the astral body, a person can explore the spiritual realm and visit other dimensions. As a result of its connection to the spiritual realm, it is considered superior to the other physical, subtle bodies.

Located one foot from the physical body, the astral body shares a special connection with the emotional body that, on occasions, both can glow the same colors.

The Etheric Template Body

This is a map of our physical self. Located about two inches away from the physical body, it is where one can find their healing power. This template was in existence long before we were.

The Celestial Body

A connection to the higher power. We can tap into this to become more aware of who we are and how we relate to everything else, forging more connections with the universe. Since it only exists in the spiritual realm, the celestial body stands out from its counterparts who exist only in the physical world. However, you can still connect to it and reach the divine when your other physical, subtle bodies are quiet. This usually happens through meditation.

The Causal Body

Last but not least is the causal body located five feet from the physical body. Referred to by some as the soul, the causal body is where all of the information about the subtle physical bodies and your awareness of being one with the divine is stored. The causal body vibrates at a higher frequency than any other subtle body with an aura of a golden color. Once you establish a connection with it, you become aware that you are one with the universe.

Have you ever wondered about people who remember their past lives? In reincarnation, your physical body does not return, but the casual body does. It carries with it the information from the subtle body, transferring it. This allows you to tap into your past lives, though you need outside help to achieve this.

The Aura

We have mentioned the aura a few times while discussing the subtle bodies, but what is the aura? Each living being is surrounded by an invisible energy field that changes colors to reflect their spiritual and emotional well-being. This energy field is the aura. Aura is invisible to the naked eye, but many people can sense other peoples' auras, often referred to as a vibe. For instance, you can meet someone and feel they "radiate" a warm and friendly vibe? What you are sensing here is their aura. You can still see your or other people's aura through peripheral vision, but it requires practice. Inside the aura is where the seven subtle bodies exist, each one forming a different layer.

Exercise

Now that you have familiarized yourself with the aura and subtle body, let us test what you have learned. As a Reiki practitioner, learning to harness energy through your hands is a skill you should master. Creating a chi ball is one of the best methods to help you focus and direct energy. You will need another person with you for this practice.

Directions
- Stand up straight
- Relax your body and mind, and inhale deeply
- Clear your thoughts and slowly exhale while focusing on your navel area. This step will help you be centered
- Now, imagine there are chords of energy stuck to your feet, acting as roots in the floor. This step will make you feel grounded and help you remain focused
- Rub your palms together until they feel warm
- Next, place your palms close together, facing each other as if you are about to clap
- Move your palms about a foot apart from each other slowly, then move them close to each other again
- Repeat this previous step a few times until you begin to feel resistance. This resistance is the energy
- Using your cupped hands, mold the energy into a ball by moving your palms back and forth
- Visualize this ball of energy as a healing light
- Make sure that the other person is sitting or lying down in a relaxed position
- Visualize the color of the healing ball. Do not overthink it, simply choose a color you feel drawn to or a mix of rainbow colors

- Set an intention for the healing ball, such as the person's name, positive thoughts, or the area of the body that requires healing
- Now place the energy ball above the other person's head
- Slowly and gently, push the ball down, visualize it entering their body, and visualize their body being filled with light
- End the exercise by silently expressing gratitude for the healing the person you helped has received

Chakras

Chakra map.
mpan, CC0, via Wikimedia Commons
https://commons.wikimedia.org/wiki/File:Chakras_map.svg

Chakras are the body's energy centers, and they first appeared in ancient Vedic texts. Chakras are the channels that distribute the life force by connecting with the Nadis. You will find this in the astral body's spine, our energy inhabiting our physical self, but this is not something tangible. The chakras move up the spine to the top of our head. Like the astral body, the chakras are invisible and cannot be touched.

There is a chakra responsible for every body part of the physical body. There are seven main chakras, and each one radiates different energy and color. Chakras can get blocked or imbalanced where the energy gets stagnant and unable to flow through the spine. Blocked chakras can manifest as symptoms affecting your body, mind, and spirit. Various things can cause a blockage to the chakras, like stress, destructive habits, or poor diet. However, changes in your lifestyle and practicing yoga, meditation, and breathing exercises can help unblock the chakras.

Root Chakra

Location: The base of the spine

Sanskrit Name: Muladhara chakra

Color: Red

Sound: Lam

Functions: The root chakra is responsible for certain bodily functions and body parts like the large intestine, bones, adrenal glands, feet, and legs. This chakra aids us in survival, safety, security, stability, and ambition. Being grounded is the main theme of this chakra which is why it is connected with anything that satisfies our basic needs, such as shelter, food, and water. The root chakra is also responsible for our basic emotional needs, such as feeling safe and secure. As human beings, meeting our basic needs can make us feel more relaxed and can greatly impact our well-being.

Symptoms of a Blocked Root Chakra

- Laziness
- Depression
- Feelings isolated and disconnected from the world
- Anxiety or panic attacks
- Nightmares
- Insecurity and feeling unsafe
- Inability to take action
- Insomnia
- Issues with the reproductive system or digestive system
- Pains and aches all over your body for no reason

- Experiencing health issues with various parts of your body like the lower back, legs, bladder, or colon

Sacral Chakra

Location: Lower abdomen. Above the pubic bone and below the navel

Sanskrit Name: Svadhishthana chakra

Color: Orange

Sound: Vam

Functions: The sacral chakra is all about having fun, which governs our sense of pleasure, passions, and all emotions related to joy. It is also connected to sexual desire and creativity. This chakra provides energy to the reproductive organs and glands, the kidneys, the circulatory system, and the bladder. When this chakra is open, you feel like your best self. You are passionate about everything in life, such as your love life and work. You also become friendly, successful, and thus fulfilled with your life. As a result, your well-being improves, and you experience feelings of joy, abundance, and wellness.

Symptoms of a Blocked Sacral Chakra

- Insecurity
- Depression
- Fatigue
- Emotional instability
- Low libido
- Fear of having pleasure or change
- Detachment
- Feeling uninspired and less creative
- Dangerous behavior like addiction
- Anemia
- PMS (premenstrual syndrome)
- Arthritis
- Less energetic
- Issues with the hips, spleen, genitals, or kidneys

- Joint pain
- Chronic pain in the lower back
- Sexual problems
- Fertility issues

Solar Plexus Chakra

Location: Lower abdomen. Between the navel and rib cage

Sanskrit Name: Manipura chakra

Color: Yellow

Sound: Ram

Functions: Confidence, personal power, willpower, and empowerment are some powerful feelings that the solar plexus chakra governs. This chakra is also responsible for the pancreas, digestive system, adrenals, and muscles.

Symptoms of a Blocked Solar Plexus Chakra

- Trust issues
- Constantly worrying about how others perceive you
- Low self-esteem
- Neediness
- Seeking approval from others
- Feeling unhealthy attachment to the people in your life
- Inability to express yourself
- Controlling behavior
- Playing the victim
- Lack of direction
- Struggling to make decisions
- Anger issues
- Procrastination
- Apathy
- Self-doubt
- Digestive issues like constipation
- Stomach aches

- Diabetes
- Eating disorders
- Ulcers
- Issues with colon, liver, and pancreas

Heart Chakra

Location: In the heart region

Sanskrit Name: Anahata chakra

Color: Green

Sound: Yam

Functions: Since this is the heart chakra, it rules over the heart and all feelings related to love, whether loving other people or self-love. As the fourth chakra, the heart chakra is in a unique position, the halfway point of the seven chakras. It bridges the upper and lower chakras to bring together their physical and spiritual aspects. This chakra is responsible for feelings of compassion, forgiveness, awareness, joy, empathy, self-love, peace, trust, generosity, change, transformation, harmony, self-acceptance, happiness, joy, motivation, and love. Simply put, it rules over many positive emotions. When open, love can flow in both directions. The heart chakra supplies energy to the heart, thymus gland, lungs, hands, and arms.

Symptoms of a Blocked Heart Chakra

- Codependency in your relationships
- Fear of rejection
- Feeling distant from the people in your life
- Trust and commitment issues
- Acting tough when feeling vulnerable
- Inability to give and receive love
- Jealousy
- Anger
- Grief
- Fear of betrayal
- Hatred towards others and yourself

- Feeling stuck and obsessed with the past
- Relationships issues
- Inability to forgive
- Feeling emotionally closed off
- Depression and anxiety
- Victim mentality
- Loneliness
- Shyness
- Lack of empathy
- Insomnia
- Asthma
- Upper back pain
- Weak immune system
- Issues with the blood circulation
- Chest pain
- Angina
- Breasts, lungs, and heart issues

Throat Chakra

Location: The throat
Sanskrit Name: Visuddha chakra
Color: Blue
Sound: Ham

Functions: Being yourself and speaking your truth are feelings associated with an open throat chakra. As the "throat" chakra, it rules over voice and communication skills. You can healthily express yourself, speak up, and truly listen to others. This chakra is also responsible for inspiring. It supplies energy to the neck, hands, shoulder, arms, parathyroid, and thyroid glands.

Symptoms of a Blocked Throat Chakra
- Shyness
- Inability to express your feelings
- Difficulty speaking up

- Aggressive behavior
- Do you feel misunderstood?
- Difficulty paying attention
- Feeling unfocused
- Worrying about what others think of you
- Sore throat
- Headaches
- Stiffness and tension in the shoulders and neck
- Thyroid difficulties

Third Eye Chakra

Location: Center of the forehead
Sanskrit Name: Ajna chakra
Color: Indigo
Sound: Aum

Functions: The third eye chakra rules over intuition. This chakra acts as a bridge between yourself and the world around you. It can also be a focal point when practicing yoga to help you remain focused and aware. When open, this chakra removes a "veil" from over our eyes that is clouding our judgment so that we can see the bigger picture. It is also connected to self-knowledge, intelligence, and insight. The third eye chakra is responsible for neurological functions, the pituitary gland, and vision.

Symptoms of a Blocked Third Eye Chakra

- Greed and only caring about material things
- Lack of purpose
- Self-doubt
- Feeling disconnected from our truest selves
- Impatience
- Depression • Feeling consumed with negative thoughts
- Narrow mindedness
- Feeling burdened with the past
- Confusion

- Lack of concentration
- Indecisiveness
- Feeling unassertive
- Fear of success
- Huge ego
- Denial
- Memory issues
- Difficulty accessing the intuition
- Inability to learn new skills
- Difficulty trusting and listening to your inner voice
- Feeling judgmental
- Feeling overwhelmed
- Anxiety and depression
- Migraines and headaches
- Dizziness
- Insomnia
- Blurry vision
- Endocrine imbalance
- Brain disorders
- Exhaustion

Crown Chakra

Location: Crown) of the head
Sanskrit Name: Sahastrara chakra
Color: Violet or white
Sound: Silence (we listen instead of chanting)

Functions: The crown chakra is the last of the seven chakras, and it rules over our spiritual connection to the divine and our higher selves. It is also considered the center of enlightenment. When open, it elevates our consciousness and makes us feel at one with the universe and connected to all its beings. As a result of being connected to the universe and the divine, we experience wisdom, self-realization, and enlightenment. It gives you a purpose in life, increases your awareness, and makes you see there is more to life than the pursuit of worldly things. The crown chakra is responsible for the central nervous system, pituitary gland, and cerebral cortex.

Symptoms of a Blocked Crown Chakra
- Sadness
- Frustration
- Destructive feelings
- Lack of inspiration
- Lacking a sense of purpose
- Apathy
- Depression
- Disconnection from the universe and all its beings
- Spiritual cynicism
- Lack of energy
- Trouble sleeping (desire to sleep all day)
- Headaches and migraines
- Exhaustion
- Destructive behavior

Exercises

Now that you have learned about the chakras, we will provide simple exercises to help you open each one.

The Root Chakra
This exercise will help you feel safe and grounded.
- Stand barefoot on the floor or grass, or sit leaning your back against a wall or a tree
- Repeat to yourself out loud, "I am safe."

The Sacral Chakra
- Find a private, quiet, and safe space
- Allow yourself to feel whatever you truly feel at this very moment. Do whatever feels right, like singing, crying, laughing, dancing, jumping, or screaming

The Solar Plexus Chakra

One of the best exercises for this chakra is to see the glass half full by looking at the brighter side of life. This will allow you to eliminate negative emotions and thoughts and replace them with positive ones.

- Buy a gratitude journal or download a gratitude journal app on your phone
- Write down one or more things or more that you are grateful for every day

This exercise will open your eyes to all the good things in your life, improving your mental health and well-being.

The Heart Chakra

To open this chakra, you need to give and receive love. This can be done by practicing visualization.

- Sit in a relaxing position in a quiet place
- Close your eyes
- Imagine someone you truly love and tell them, "they deserve to be loved and happy."
- Now imagine someone you are mad at, and tell them the same thing
- Lastly, imagine you are also telling yourself you deserve to be loved

The Throat Chakra

To open this chakra, you should speak your truth and express yourself. Focus on finding your voice and clearly communicating your thoughts. You can do this gradually and in one-on-one situations first. Start with the people closest to you and whom you are comfortable around until you are ready to express yourself to more people. If you need to speak your truth, do it. Train yourself never to stay silent when you have something to say unless it is inappropriate or you are angry (when it is better to remain silent!)

The Third Eye Chakra

The best exercise for this chakra is candle-gazing meditation.

- Sit in a dark and quiet room
- Light a candle

- Gaze at the candle while breathing deeply for a few minutes
- Close your eyes so they can adjust. Then when you are ready, open them and go on with your day

The Crown Chakra

This chakra is about finding your purpose in life and increasing your self-awareness. The best exercise here is to get to know yourself better. Through journaling, ask yourself questions and answer them. You can also download an app with interesting questions that will help you learn so much about yourself.

Learning everything about the subtle bodies and chakras will pave the way to mastering and manipulating energy. Take your time and practice the exercises we have mentioned daily to help you advance as a practitioner.

Chapter 3: Meditation and Visualization

Part-I: MEDITATION

What Is Meditation?

Meditation is the art of calming the mind. It is used to promote relaxation, build inner strength, and is the art of concentrating on a single object or point. It involves sitting quietly, focusing on your breath, and reciting a mantra or prayer.

Meditation and visualization.
https://pixabay.com/es/photos/meditar-lago-estado-animico-4882027/

Meditation helps slow down our minds because they work 24/7, and thoughts keep racing through our minds. Thoughts can be about important issues or could be you overthinking things and disturbing your internal peace. Meditation can be practiced at any time in a peaceful environment to focus and relax.

Different Types of Meditation

There are many different kinds of meditation techniques performed worldwide, and you are bound to find one which resonates with you and your needs. The point of meditation is to reach mental peace and physical relaxation.

1. Guided Meditation

This is the type of meditation performed to achieve certain things. It can be your work achievement, weight, peace, or health. In this mediation, we focus and visualize imagery of what we want to achieve. Guided meditation also helps get rid of mental blocks to see the clarity of things.

2. Tartak Meditation

This technique helps to focus on things. This type of meditation is performed when we want to focus on work but can't - due to distractions. In this style of meditation, we focus on one point, place, or candle flame as long as possible to improve our concentration level.

3. Transcended Meditation

This meditation is where a word, sound, or phrase is repeated or received until your mind transcends into a different world.

4. Mindfulness Meditation

Mindfulness meditation is adopted from Buddhist meditation. In this, we focus on present moments and on inhales and exhales of breathing. It is a simple meditative technique, and anyone can do it quite easily.

A Simple Method to Meditate

There are many techniques to meditation, but if we look at a simple meditation practice, we can not go wrong with mindfulness meditation. Root yourself in the present, and pay attention to what is around you.

To perform this meditation, we must follow some basic and simple steps.

1. The first thing that you need to do is to find a comfortable position. Finding a peaceful and comfortable position to perform this meditation is wise because distraction can ruin the purpose of this meditation. But it is not necessary to find a place outside your house. You can do it in your room, office, or any other quiet and peaceful place.

2. Many yogis recommend performing the meditation in a certain leg and hand position at a certain angle, but it is simple meditation, and for beginners as well, so it does not matter which leg position you are following. You must cross your legs comfortably and put your hands on your knees or lap.

3. Keep your back straight during meditation. However, if you suffer from injury or pain or have just started your meditation journey, you can place a pillow on your back or lean against the wall.

4. The fourth step is to close your eyes and focus on one thing. Breathe in and out, focusing on your breathing. Experience your chest moving in and out. While doing this, feel your chest, shoulder, belly, or anything that feels appropriate. It is okay to have thoughts while meditating, but one should struggle to overcome those distractions to better focus.

5. Ideally, it is recommended to meditate for at least 20 minutes a day. However, if you are a beginner, you can meditate for a few minutes, set a timer, and see how much time you can meditate in a day. Increase the time by one minute a day until you reach the recommended 20 -30 minutes.

Mindfulness meditation also helps in spiritual awakening, so keep a positive mindset and be patient during meditation.

Master the Breathing Technique

When practicing meditation, especially mindfulness meditation, it is important to focus on your breath.

To master the breathing techniques during meditation, you first need to sit straight and firmly on the ground. The position of your knees and hips should be at a 90-degree angle, and your back should be straight. However, if you have an injury or are experiencing pain, you can lean on the wall or support your back with a pillow or cushion.

Start by taking deep, natural breaths without altering or controlling them. After taking a breath at a natural rhythm, take a deep breath through the nose and feel that breath into your body.

Feel the expanding and contraction of the lungs as you inhale and exhale, and feel the breath in your belly and other body parts. Take another deep breath and repeat the process a few times.

Now take a deep breath from your nose and exhale through your month.

When you take a deep breath from your nose, you'll feel a warm sensation of air on the upper mouth area and coolness when it releases.

Continue the process of warmness and coolness of the air in your nostrils for a few minutes. After completion, bring back your attention slowly and gently open your eyes.

Several Benefits of Meditation

Meditation helps you slow down the number of thoughts that are affecting your mental health and physical capabilities. Meditation increases positive emotions and helps to control emotions like anger or grief. It helps to increase the ability to focus and concentrate.

Deep breathing during meditation helps stay clear, strengthening the immune system. It helps to cure depression and also helps in spiritual awakening. It also decreases anxiety, stress, and pain.

1. A Gateway to Psychic Energy

Meditation is a powerful tool that helps to grow psychic capabilities. Everyone can develop psychic abilities through meditation.

When we meditate, we clear our minds and focus more on our breathing. Meditation gives you a heightened awareness and helps you connect to your center and create energy inside your body.

Many people take meditation as a tool, a primary purpose for relaxation and de-stress, and focusing more, but that is all a by-product of meditation. Meditation helps you get rid of anger, greed, and delusion. When we meditate, we get rid of all things, creating internal energy in us to go on a path of spiritual enlightenment.

2. Make Energy Healing (Reiki) Possible

Defined in simple terms, Reiki is universal energy we get through meditation. It is a Japanese style of channeling energy through the whole body. This energy gives immersive relief and also helps to connect with spirit guides. Spirit guides only connect and communicate with humans if they have high energy and frequency, and Reiki helps to develop that energy.

Reiki meditation is performed by sitting in a quiet place with a specific position of hands at specific points on the body. It helps cure depression and anxiety and brings more focus and a calm mind.

3. The Gassho Prayer

Dr. Mikao Usui created the Gassho prayer technique, and the prayer word translates as: "two hands coming together."

To perform Gassho's prayer, you need to sit calmly with a straight back and closed eyes and sit in the position just as we do in meditation. Position your hands in the prayer position placing the hands and palms together in the "Namaste" position in front of the hand chakra.

If you are distracted by something, you could press your middle fingertips gently to refocus attention and get rid of thoughts.

Take deep breaths and do this for 15-30 minutes. You can start with five minutes daily if you are just a beginner. This helps you focus more, purifies your mind and heart, and brings out positivity.

Part-II: VISUALIZATION
What Is Visualization?

Visualization is a technique that focuses and calms the mind while also promoting creativity and problem-solving skills. Visualization is a thought process. We think about something first in our mind – and then manifest it into the physical plane.

The goal of visualization is to create images in the mind that are positive and relaxing, to achieve a state of relaxation and focus, and help to move energy within the body.

Five Techniques to Visualize

While it may take a while before you get accustomed to this process, there are five basic techniques to get started with visualization.

Technique # 1. Color Breathing

This type of visualization helps relieve stress and brings positive vibes and a good mood.

1. For this, you need to consider a color you like.
2. Sit in a comfortable position, just as you do in meditation. Now, close your eyes and take deep breaths, placing all of your attention on your breathing.
3. Then, visualize the color you have chosen. Choose the color you may be feeling right now or one which will give you soothing vibes.
4. Take deep breaths while holding that color in your mind. Imagine breathing and spreading this color throughout your body in the form of light into all parts of your body. If, at any time, thoughts, images, or sounds come to mind during visualization, acknowledge them and gently ignore them.
5. When you breathe out, visualize that you are breathing out stress and worries

Continue this visualization and breathing process as long as you want to lighten the relevant body part.

Technique # 2. Compassion Meditation Visualization

Compassion Meditation helps you to understand the suffering of others and their feelings and to feel love for them. Compassion Meditation visualization leads to improved moods, good behavior, and less anger and greed. Below are the steps to follow:

1. To start, get yourself comfortable. Close your eyes and breathe in and out, feeling yourself breathe. Take deep breaths in natural places without forcing yourself.
2. Then visualize the person you want to send love, grief, and compassion to. It can be a loved one or your own pets or animals.
3. Picture them in your thoughts and think about how you feel about them, whether you have a love for them or want to be compassionate to them in their pain. Be deliberate and true about the feeling you want to send. Imagine the feeling in your mind, and surround that feeling with a golden light.
4. Use these words: "The pain is going; the peace is coming." Remember to breathe as you chant this. Focus on the golden feeling you imagined and see it leaving your body. It is traveling to the person who needs it. You can also retain the golden feeling if you need the healing.
5. After completing this, you'll fill love and freedom from pain. Repeat this visualization as needed.

Technique # 3. Progressive Muscle Relaxation

This muscle visualization exercise helps you release muscle tension and stiffness due to anxiety or stress. Below are the exact steps to follow:

1. Find a comfortable position.
2. Take a slow deep breath through your nostrils, and hold it for a few seconds.
3. Again, take a deep breath, close your eyes, and tighten your forehand and mouth muscles. After five seconds, exhale it while visualizing the tension leaving your body.
4. Again, take a deep breath while squeezing the muscles of your hands for five minutes. Imagine you are squeezing a lemon for lemonade.

5. Exhale and visualize that all the tension is released from your body as exhaling the air out.
6. Take a slow, deep breath again while squeezing the shoulder muscles for five seconds, and try to touch your ears with your shoulder.
7. Repeat the same inhalation and exhalation process in all of your muscles

Technique # 4. Guided Imagery

Guided imagery helps you to release stress and cure depression by visualizing images, scenery, and positive pictures.

1. For this, sit comfortably and close your eyes, just as in meditation.
2. Inhale deeply and visualize the scenery or images with each breath.
3. When you want to exhale, visualize the stress, unmanageable feelings, and anxiety leaving your body

Technique # 5. Goals visualization

The technique of goals visualization is used to imagine your goals or secure your future. In this meditation, visualize their future or goals and create a scene in imagination.

1. Visualize your success. See your goal in your mind in great detail, and see yourself achieving it.
2. If some negative thoughts appear, recite the mantra and keep faith in yourself.
3. Take a slow, deep breath, exhale, and visualize your success or goals.

With these techniques, you can explore the realm of visualization and find the one that suits you best.

Habits to Promote Visualization

1. Avoiding the Habit of Overthinking

To practice visualization, it is important not to overthink. During meditation and visualization, distractions occur.

For instance, in visualization, if you are practicing color breathing or image visualization and want to focus on one box or color, your brain might start to overthink the shape of the box or which color to choose, etc. This type of distraction ruins the purpose of visualization.

However, it is normal to overthink, and you can slowly overcome it by practicing visualization regularly.

2. Using All Your Senses

Use all of your scenes to get more benefit from visualization. For example, try to use all senses if you imagine some scenery or image. Try to feel, smell, and use your body in that scenario. It will boost the visualization, and you'll benefit from it.

3. Parting Ways with Judgements

In visualization, it is important not to judge or compare yourself to others. The mind is a chatterbox, and it keeps thinking round the clock, which is quite exhausting.

Many necessary or unusual thoughts appear in your mind. For instance, during visualization, you suddenly start to think about your to-do list or upcoming work instead of visualizing. Try not to judge yourself because everything takes time, and you can focus more on visualization if you practice daily.

4. Stay Relaxed While Practicing

The foremost step in visualization is to relax, sit in a comfortable position, and have a peaceful environment that calms your mind. Practice visualization daily. Start with five minutes each day and then increase the period by one minute daily.

Various Benefits of Visualization

There are many overlapping advantages of meditation and visualization, leading to some people becoming confused between the two. Visualization has some distinct benefits that highlight its significance and positive impact. Below are some of its benefits:

1. It helps in reducing stress and enhances focus and clarity. In short, it optimizes the overall functioning of your senses. In this manner, it is a great tool for artists or writers.
2. Visualization also provides great emotional stability and may even promote the spirit of kindness.
3. Once you start practicing "visualization," you'll notice a substantial improvement in your sleep quality and boost your immune system.
4. In addition, it helps bring positive energy to the body. It also enhances creativity and builds problem-solving skills.

That said, meditation and visualization go hand in hand, and you cannot separate the two if you truly want to experience a deep positive impact.

Chapter 4: Working with Your Guides

Spirit guides are the universal forces that help protect, love, and guide us towards wisdom. They are our companions and our divine parents. They are with us before we are even born and can take any form.

The way spirit guides appear or present themselves to us is based on what we believe. They can be in the form of Angels, Animals, Ancestors, Ancients, plants, or any form that has significance to you. Spirit guides are here to help us. Their main purpose is to teach or comfort us, but they also help us learn about ourselves and show us the right path to grow.

Different Types of Spirit Guides

There are many types of spirit guides, and we have listed a few below, together with a brief description.

1. **Angel Spirit Guides**

Guardian angels are here to teach us valuable lessons, guide us through our hardships, and help us differentiate between right and wrong.

They are non-denominational; subsequently, they protect and guide people of all beliefs and faiths. We all have more than one Guardian Angel. They are known as the "awakened ones," and if we call them spiritually, they will guide us.

2. Animal Spirit Guides

Animals are well-known powerful spirit guides. They are raw and pure. Sometimes, they are pets who have passed on and come back to aid you.

We can also have spiritual guidance through animals around us. For example, bears teach us how to be strong and confident, butterflies show us how we can change ourselves into a better people, cats show us how to be independent, and dogs teach us how to stay loyal and show unconditional love to our loved ones, and owls show us wisdom.

Butterflies are an example of animal spirit guides.
https://pixabay.com/es/photos/mariposas-flores-polinizar-1127666/

We can take spiritual guidance from animals around us by spending time outside and focusing on the unusual behavior of animals which sometimes appear, again and again, paying attention to every activity around us. They teach us the lesson of empowerment, how to let go of small things, and lessons of love and joy.

3. Ancestors as Spirit Guides

Departed loved ones can also be your spirit guides. They can support you from heaven and show you the right path, whether your career path or life journey.

They can be anyone, whether you have a blood connection with them or not. Any human who passes can become your spirit guide who was once in the same position as yours and now wants to help you out from that.

4. Masters as Spirit Guides

Masters like Buddha are the ultimate teachers. They are enlightened ones and give guidance and teach us during the journey of spiritual awakening. They work as leaders or teachers in the spirit world and help us connect with the divine.

5. Protection Spirit Guides

Protection spirit guides or helper angels help humans in their difficulties. They give signals and signs to warn humans about dangerous situations they might face in the future. They protect and help them in their daily chores.

6. Light Beings

This is another name for a guardian angel, but people don't always like to use the term angel. They are spirits who help guide people through difficult situations or recover from traumatic events. They will likely be shrouded in light to both literally and metaphorically guide you down the right path.

How to Work with Spirit Guides

Spirit guides, our guardians, and our protectors are easy to connect and communicate with, but you should have inner belief in them. They can not interfere in your life until you ask them.

Spirit guide helpers or angels exist on higher frequency levels, and we can not necessarily see them with our physical eyes. Yet, they can communicate with us through symbols and signs and establish connections to yourself and your heart.

To visualize yourself with the spirit guides, you must imagine yourself at a higher frequency and energy level. Once you are at an aligned frequency, the spirit guides will respond to your call. However, if you are unable to tune into their energy levels, your spirit guide will not be able to hear your message.

The average frequency level of a human being is 62 to 75 **MHz**, and if you are feeling unwell, you'll notice your frequency level will fall below 62MHz. The higher the frequency level, the higher the chances they can hear you.

All divine angels help and guide us, but you need to be alert to their signals which can sometimes be very subtle. A spirit guide will find ways to communicate; it is a human's job to listen to them.

Everyone has angels - a team of spirit guides ready to help when asked. Try to interpret their message, create a language, a way to communicate with them because they will find ways to help you, but one should be able to tune into their intuition.

A Simple Way to Connect with Them

Spiritual guides speak in silence, or they give us signals and signs. The signs might be a physical sign or message.

Keep your mind conscious but separate it from the outside world to connect with them. The mind is super active. It keeps thinking of things, upcoming works, and many other life problems. The more thoughts in your mind, the less it can listen and focus on spirit guides.

The mind works like a filter that separates the outside world and illusion. You must keep your mind conscious and try to communicate with your spiritual guide.

Practice the Art of Meditation

Meditation helps connect spirit guides.
https://www.pexels.com/photo/fashion-people-woman-relaxation-8391315/

Meditation can help to connect with them through the conscious mind. It generates internal peace and lets you keep worries and problems out of your mind so you can easily communicate with your spirit's guides.

To meditate, find a nice, calm, and peaceful environment where no outside source or voice can disturb you. Try to calm your body, sit comfortably with closed eyes, and play mantras or prayers for five to ten minutes.

Through this conscious period, you'll feel many things. Set a goal of two to three weeks, as you probably will not feel something right away because spiritual guidance depends upon the energy and belief level.

There is another level of consciousness that is the heart.

When you can connect with your spirit guides easily, you'll see *after that time* that you'll not receive any signals or signs – and you do not need to call your spirit guides to help you. Instead, your heart is giving signals, telling you what is right and wrong or which path is best for you. This happens because you have reached a higher level of spiritual awakening, and Angel, or master or spirit guide, is within you.

Another important part of connecting with your guides is allowing them to help you out in your life. You can allow them into your life by permitting them. Permit them aloud or in your heart. You can also write a note in a journal.

After allowing them, ask them for message reinforcement, ask them to reinforce the message into 3D reality, physical signs, and messages.

The quieter your mind is, the easier it will be to connect with your spirit guides. Stay present, keep your mind conscious in looking at and observing the outside world, and don't miss the messages. Sometimes, spirit guides give message signals repeatedly, but your mind doesn't receive them because it is not paying attention to the messages. Make sure to keep your mind conscious after asking for help.

Spirit guides can also appear in your dreams. Before going to bed, relax and ask them to appear in dreams or send you signals in your dreams. Again, they will not instantly appear, but try again and again and put maximum energy and consciousness into asking.

You can also connect with them through tarots. You can read tarots on your own or get someone to read them for you. Playing soothing music and exercising will also help you connect with spirit guides.

Signs That They Are Communicating

Spirit guides communicate with us in subtle ways to help us in certain aspects of life. They can send us signs in many ways, and it is up to us how much we are spiritually awakened to understand them.

1. **Vivid Dreams**

Spirit guides sometimes create vivid scenarios and convey their messages through dreams and visions. However, it can happen that when you wake up, you completely forget the dream, so to remember it, write down as much as you remember in a journal and try to focus on which signal your spirit guide has given to you.

2. **Intuition**

Spirit guides often send us messages through intuition. We can hear strong telephonic voices or strong gut feelings for certain kinds of work or people.

These signals are for spirit guides to help and guide you from difficult situations.

3. Music

Music is a universal language with a higher frequency level that helps spirit guides to communicate with us.

If you suddenly saw or heard some old music or lyrics that have some connections with your life, then it might be a signal from spirit guides.

4. Repeated Numbers

If you see repeated numbers, quotes, or phrases, then your spirit guides could be trying to connect with you through written materials and give a message repeatedly.

5. Touch

If you feel any light-weight touches on your neck, shoulders, or head and a sensation that someone is either there accompanying or watching you, then you do not need to be afraid because spiritual guides are providing you consultation.

Other signs include smell, a sudden nice and pleasant smell that reminds you of your past or any important event.

White feathers are also a sign from spiritual guides. It indicates the sign of luck. It can be found in the strangest places that you might not accept, but if you see white feathers, consider it a sign from your spirit guides.

Benefits of Having Spirit Guides

Spirit guides are positive incorporeal entities that guide and offer assistance to living human beings. And by connecting with them, you can connect between two different worlds, the materialistic one and the spiritual one.

1. Guidance

Spirit Guides are guardians of the soul. They provide us with the right path and help us in our life's ups and downs. They will guide us through our whole life span.

One should have faith in their spirit guide and thank them after guidance.

2. Support

They are a support system. By connecting with them, you'll never feel alone. They will be with you in any obstacles and guide and support you.

They are navigators of life and can help us in our relationship or friendship issues and career path and protect us from making wrong decisions.

3. Master

They become masters or mentors of our life once we connect with them. Spirit guides are the best companions and best friends of human beings.

They help you deal with the outside world, and by having their friendship on your side, you can easily face any hurdles in your life because they mentor and teach you in every phase of life.

4. Protections

They protect every aspect of life and from any bad things. To protect ourselves from bad things, we should focus on things happening around us because guidance continuously gives signals to us.

If you do not feel good intentions from something or someone, stay away from that because it might be a signal from Spirit guides.

How Do They Complement a Psychic Reiki Session?

Reiki guides the universal energy that is in all of us. In this process, therapists can channel energy into patients' bodies to activate natural healing and spiritual awakening.

Reiki is performed to ease pain and depression, and relaxation of one's body and helps to filter out the mind from unusual thoughts.

To connect with your spirit guides, it is essential to call them by using energy and a higher frequency. The higher the energy level, the sooner they will respond. But sudden blockage will affect upon calling them, and Reiki is often performed to remove the sudden blockage from the body.

Reiki is often performed by placing hands in specific positions. You might feel sudden pressure on the chest and tingling in your arms and legs during this. This sensation indicates the blockage of energy. During Reiki, the body will release stress and depression and return to its natural state.

Sudden pressure and tingling signify that your body is reaching its natural state and removing its blockage.

Reiki transfers positive energy to patients so they can focus more on current events. Reiki clarifies the mind and helps you concentrate on the problems and opportunities in your life. By focusing on current events, you'll likely catch a sign or message from Spiritual Gods.

Reiki helps in sleeping better. After a reiki session, your body will feel completely relaxed and tension-free, which will help you sleep and heal better, and a peaceful sleep means more chances of vivid dreams that give you signs and guide you.

Helps with Harmony and Balance

Reiki moves the energy around your body, unblocking blockages and sending the energy where it needs to go—creating balance. This includes all of the body systems and creates an environment of harmony conducive to a balanced lifestyle.

Reiki helps you with physical relaxation. It helps your body to go into its natural state. It helps you focus on whatever you are trying to put your energy into.

Reiki originated in Japan in 2000 and was later introduced around the globe. As it moved further around the world, the art was further developed. Reiki is not only hand movement but can be a pet therapy, music, deep breathing, and much more. All of this therapy can be a meditative spiritual awakening.

A Reiki session is performed to calm the mind and help in spiritual awakening.

In reiki sessions, besides hand massage, music is often used to relax your mind. This therapy is called Karuna therapy. During this therapy, therapists play soothing music, a record of nature, and audio sounds to transmit energy and positive messages in your body.

Another psychic reiki session includes rainbow Reiki. In this session, seven main chakras in the body are used to bring healing. This spiritual bringing is used to heal and understand the nature and things around us.

Aromatic reiki sessions also help in spiritual awakening. A reiki session combined with aromatherapy oils is a great relaxer and also brings pleasure. Aromatherapy oils have strong scents that link to the person, their past life, or any special events. Through this, the person can be focused more on past events and focus on spiritual guides.

Many ways and many other types of Reiki complement and initiate the spiritual awakening of human beings.

Chapter 5: Clearing and Grounding

The world around us is wired with energy, both good and bad. The people we interact with and the tools or objects we use daily have energy fields and auras. What you may not notice is that these things have a significant impact on our own energies, as strong vibrations can easily attract us toward them. This is why regular energy clearing is essential. It allows us to identify our own vibrational frequency and guarantee that our inner aura flows smoothly.

Energy clearing can help us eliminate intrusive thoughts and emotions, allowing us to maintain a positive outlook on life. Since energy is supposed to flow, attempting to suppress the negativity or push it to the back of our minds only creates added problems. Clearing can allow you to let unhelpful vibrations flow outside the mind and body. This practice's effects are not experienced immediately but are felt gradually. The more you practice the techniques, the more you'll get the hang of it. It requires a lot of determination, focus, and, most importantly, patience.

Picture the world itself as one enormous battery. It is naturally charged with its own unique, subtle energy. It ensures our stability, protection, and safety. Everything electrical, whether it is a television or our bodies, is connected to the Earth. This is what we know as being "grounded." Practicing grounding can help diminish stress and tension and promote positive energies like strength and balance. We feel centered when we are grounded and experience fewer physical pain and symptoms.

The physical symptoms we experience are not as upfront as we think. Let us take headaches, for example. Most people do not think much of this seemingly min0r ailment. They take a pain reliever and call it a day. However, what they do not realize is that their physical condition can be a manifestation of a hindrance in their energetic flow. Headaches could be a sign of stress, uncertainty, a lack of mental clarity, an abundance of negative thoughts, and more. This is why headaches usually accompany the compelling need to just step away from everything. We should never ignore our physical symptoms because, in most cases, our bodies are trying to tell us something. Indulging in a stress-relieving activity or practicing a hobby can help you raise your vibrations and release the accumulated negative energies.

Any type of healing work must be preceded by energy clearing and grounding. In this chapter, we will explain what clearing and grounding are. We will also review some techniques you can use to cleanse your energy and center yourself.

What Is Energy Clearing?

Many confuse "energy healing" and "energy clearing." While it may sound like both of them refer to the same process, the concepts are very different. You can not start the healing process unless you have cleared your energy. Healing your energy is concerned with all types of imbalances. After all, energy is the foundation of everything. Even intangibles, such as emotions, thoughts, and our spiritual side, are all energy. Energy clearing, on the other hand, refers to certain situations. Sometimes, you'll find yourself someplace or dealing with something with an energy that no longer serves you. In that case, you would take remedial action, energy clearing, to release these negative energies.

Do I Need to Clear My Energy?

Anyone with a blockage in their vibrational energy needs to practice energy clearing activities. But how can you work out if you need to clear your energy?

The following are some telltale signs that your energy needs to be cleared:

- You struggle with insomnia, poor quality of sleep, or other sleep problems.
- You are drained, depressed, stressed, anxious, or lethargic for no apparent reason.
- You are always fatigued even after sleeping well through the night.
- You are suddenly experiencing a wide range of health problems, whether simultaneously or one after the other. Examples include physical pain, muscle tension, stiffness, headaches, lethargy, dizziness, etc.
- You always sense negativity in the air. There is a constant feeling that something bad is happening or going to happen.
- Something feels off, but you just can not lay a finger on what the problem may be.
- You can not shake negative feelings, vibes, or impressions regarding a place, situation, or person.
- You can not sit or stand still, especially if this is atypical behavior. You're always restless or fidgeting around.
- You are in stagnant energy, or you feel stuck.
- Your emotions are all over the place, or you experience extreme shifts or sudden hits of emotions without clear or compelling reasons.
- You are unproductive, unable to control your thoughts, experiencing brain fog, or your mind and actions are going in circles.
- You need to clear your energy if you notice that your energy is off and you cannot pinpoint what is causing the problem.

Clearing Energies

Bubble of Light

The "Bubble of Light" technique is among the most popular energy clearing practices, primarily because it is easy and effective. This method can be practiced while standing up, sitting, or lying down.

Get into a comfortable position and close your eyes. Focus on your center. Imagine that there is a small, harmless flame there. The flame is white, and as you dwell on it, it becomes brighter and stronger. You are going to ask this flame to protect your body. It is going to stop outside influences from damaging you. Visualize the gradual growth of this flame until it lights up your entire body. Once you see that this light has filled you, urge it to penetrate your skin, making its way to your energy body.

This practice can be done daily or when you feel you need it. It can come in handy when there is plenty of energy in the air. Excuse yourself from overwhelming family gatherings, vehement meetings, arguments, or other unpleasant interactions to complete this practice. If that is not possible, doing it afterward can help you release unwanted energies.

Namaste Hands

The chances are that you have heard of the popular yoga practice where the practitioners bring their hands together and say "namaste." It is perhaps the most common Hindu and Buddhist valediction. What you may not know, however, is that this practice holds a much deeper meaning.

When you think about it, the essence of yoga is to clear and restructure the energy and space within the physical, spiritual, emotional, and mental aspects of your being. After the time and effort you have dedicated to letting go of what no longer serves you to make the space for positivity, you can create a symbolic circle to close in these efforts by bringing your hands together. Placing your flat palms parallel to your heart helps you confirm that what you have released remains outside your body, and everything you have attracted and built stays safely inside. While it is ideally practiced after another healing or clearing activity, you can reap its benefits by doing it at any time and place. However, bringing your hands together in front of your arms in a public setting would seem weird. Sitting at a table, you can do it under its surface. The heart plays a significant symbolic role. But the hand and touch are more powerful. Doing it whenever there is a lot of undesired energy hanging around allows you to declare that nothing will go in or go out without your permission. Our palms have receptive and expressive centers that serve as barriers.

Cording

Cording is an age-old practice that is influenced by shamanic practices. Ironically, this technique feels a lot like a de-cording practice that clears the energy and protects and contains it. Cords refer to energetic bonds and connections that an individual cultivates with another person, a group of people, a place, a habit, an idea, an emotional wound, or even an object. It is called a cord because it is not just a connection but a vehicle that enables energy exchange between both entities. The energy given or received is not always equally reciprocated. In toxic relationships, your energy is drained and never replenished.

As we have just explained, a cord is formed when you build a connection with another entity. Cords can also be formed if another person attaches them to you, even when you do not attempt to forge the same connection. A teacher does so with their students, and authors do that with readers. These cords can either be attached maliciously due to hatred, disgust, or jealousy or positively as a reflection of admiration and respect. Either way, these cords are out of your scope of control, leaving you unable to control your own energy. For instance, people who can not get over their past relationships usually try to re-cultivate these cords. More often than not, this creates a harmful effect. The best way to remedy this situation would be by practicing this technique.

Start with the Mountain Pose and slowly allow your eyes to shut. See the energy flowing through your body—it is all connected. Move from the top of your head to the tips of your toes. As you do so, imagine yourself plucking these cords and releasing them from your body. Go over your energy body, plucking all the cords three times. Then, end your practice with the "Bubble of Light" exercise.

Reiji Ho

Reiji Ho is a Reiki energy clearing technique. Unlike other standard Reiki hand poses, this particular method is more intuitive. It helps its practitioners locate imbalances and encourage balance, creating energetic healing opportunities.

To practice this technique, sit comfortably and bring your hands to Gassho, or prayer position. Close your eyes and bring your attention to the hard center in your lower belly or abdomen. Stay focused on your breathing. Activate Reiki, allowing its energy to flow throughout your entire body, making its way to all of your cells. Envision it filling you up and the space around you.

Move your hands to your forehead, requesting holistic healing. Do not guide your hands, but let them make their way toward the areas in your body that need healing. Do not supervise the process nor disrupt it. Where your hands stop, allow them to pass on the positive energies. You can intuitively tell when you have finished a certain area or the entire process. When you are done, rest your palms on your lap. Take a few breaths and acknowledge your gratitude.

How to Clear the Energy

Smudging

Smudging is a very effective energy clearing technique. It is known to have various health benefits due to its antimicrobial qualities. It is also proven to positively influence the mood and aid with insomnia.

Keep a door or window open as you practice this technique. This serves as a safety measure and a gateway for negative energies to leave your space. Start by setting your intentions regarding the things you wish to release and cleanse your space. Come up with a relevant prayer or mantra you can repeat throughout the process. A simple mantra would be, "I let go of what doesn't serve me." Now that you are ready, hold the sage at approximately a 45-degree angle and light it using a candle or match. Allow it to burn for 20 seconds before blowing out the flame. You should see orange embers before the smoke billows upward. Walk slowly around the space to spread the smoke around, gently guiding it and the negative energy toward the door or window. To extinguish the sage, press it firmly onto a fireproof surface.

Use a Singing Bowl

Sounds, especially bells, can absorb negative energies and drive them away. Singing bowls have pure, bell-like, resonating tones that can help energy levels fall into balance. To use this instrument, you need to position it gently onto the palm of your hands. Bring your awareness to how it feels and its weight on your hands. When you are ready, strike the rim of the bowl gently a couple of times to familiarize yourself with its sound. Start playing it freely, allowing the energies to flow into your body. Move around, so it fills up your space. In each place you go, strike it three times, and bring your awareness to the tone that it makes. Some places will cause a dull sound, while others will allow for the generation of more lively sounds, reflecting the energies in different places. Focus on ringing the bowl near walls, windows, and doors. You can move the mallet in a clockwise circle over the rim as an alternative to striking the bowl.

What Is Grounding?

Grounding is a therapeutic practice that is alternatively known as "earthing." Practicing this technique requires you to ground yourself and cultivate a strong electrical connection with the earth. Grounding physics and earthing science are scientific fields concerned with how electric charges from the Earth can positively influence one's body. It is very important to note that the grounding techniques used to aid in coping with mental health issues are different from these types of grounding techniques.

Anyone can practice grounding techniques. They are very beneficial when it comes to tuning and balancing the physical and spiritual energies in our being. Grounding allows you to shift your consciousness to the present, physical moment. This promotes a steady and centered energy, making you more focused and mentally stronger.

How to Ground Yourself

Tree Root

Go out in nature and find a safe, quiet space to stand or sit barefoot on the ground. Keep your feet flat on the ground and take deep breaths, focusing on how the earth feels underneath you. Visualize your feet growing roots that make their way to Earth's center. Breathe in deeply from the roots, pulling the energy through your soles and into your body. Allow it to traverse your being, nourishing you in the process. Imagine the stress making its way out of the crown of your head. Raise your arms and visualize them as long tree branches. Reach up to feel the warmth of the sun. Feed off the relaxing energies of the sun and earth.

Use Healing Crystals

Wear or carry with you a healing crystal to ground yourself. Bear in mind that each healing crystal serves a different purpose. Choose carnelian, bloodstone, gold tiger eye, hematite, amber, pyrite, or garnet when it comes to grounding.

Earthing

Take a walk barefoot on sand, grass, or dirt. This will help you reinvigorate your energy.

You can think of energy as a spectrum with a light end and a very dark one. Compassion, care, love, and other positive vibrations fall into the light side of the spectrum. Hatred, fear, and similar low and negative vibrations lie on the dark side of the spectrum. Everything in the world, including humans and inanimate objects, constantly sends out and receives energy. This is why we must reflect on our daily life and interactions to monitor these energy exchanges before we embark on the healing journey.

Chapter 6: Developing Your Psychic Abilities

Have you ever wondered how tarot and oracle readers gather all the information they need to give their clients a better understanding of their reality and insights into what is in store for them? The key here is nothing more than the four clairs of intuition. Psychics and readers constantly work on developing and strengthening their intuition. When you are highly intuitive, you can easily grasp what is trying to be communicated to you. The four clairs are known as clairaudience, which means "clear hearing," clairvoyance, meaning "clear seeing," clairsentience refers to "clear feelings," and claircognizance, which is "clear knowing."

Some people are born with naturally stronger clairs. It is not uncommon to find someone who has very strong clairsentience but weak clairvoyant abilities. There are many online quizzes you can take to discover your strongest clair. Fortunately, you can also do many things to improve your overall psychic and intuitive abilities.

In this chapter, we will explore the four clairs in more depth. Then, you'll find various tips and techniques for developing and refining your psychic abilities.

Intuition and Psychics

Did you know that to a certain degree, we are all psychic? We all have natural intuitive abilities. However, we tend to disregard them or underestimate them, particularly because we have very high expectations regarding what psychic abilities should be. We are all tricked into believing that psychic abilities are more complex and harder to achieve than they are. This is why most people think they are completely lofty and out of reach; therefore, they never attempt to strengthen them.

While not everyone wants to be psychic, a few realize that developing their intuitive abilities can serve them in numerous aspects of life. We experience the impact of intuition every day. Do you know why you feel oddly uncomfortable around a specific person? Or how you walk into a room and get an ill vibe? That is your intuition coming into play.

Our intuition is what safeguards us from potential harm or hurt. It instills our confidence in our knowledge, allowing us to make better and faster decisions. Our inner voice, or gut feeling, extends beyond normal logic and reason. It allows us to combine the information we have with who we essentially are so we can act accordingly. Intuition is also associated with heightened creativity, which fosters greater opportunities.

If you wish to pull cards, complete tarot readings, or are just interested in heightening your senses and easing your daily experiences, you should consider working on your intuitive abilities.

What Are the Clairs?

There are eight clair senses that we can tap into to receive unearthly information:

1. **Clairvoyance** – clear seeing
2. **Clairaudience** – clear hearing
3. **Claircognizance** – clear knowing
4. **Clairsentience** – clear feeling
5. **Clairgustance** – clear tasting
6. **Clairsalience** – clear smelling

7. **Clairempathy** - clear emotions
8. **Clairtangency** - clear touch

However, the first four clairs, which we will discuss in more depth, are the most important. They are indispensable when it comes to seeking guidance on our paths of growth and transformation. Focusing on these four can help us heighten our collective consciousness. Developing these clair abilities allows you to raise your empathy and intuition, which helps you nurture your relationships and improve your decision-making abilities.

Clairvoyance

When the word psychic comes up, most people immediately imagine a woman staring into a crystal ball, waiting for her client's future to unfold right before her eyes. This stereotype is perhaps the reason behind the term *clairvoyant*, which is believed to be synonymous with the word psychic. Many people don't realize that clairvoyance is just one of the numerous clairs and tools that a psychic uses.

A psychic receives clairvoyant messages or downloads as scenes, colors, dreams, visions, or imagery in their minds, or even externally, with their eyes. These messages aren't always straightforward and are often metaphorical. Yes, kind of like dreams!. For instance, an overwhelmed or stressed client may appear to be drowning. If someone is experiencing major life changes, the psychic may see the ground shaking beneath their feet. Fishing represents the search for new opportunities. Different readers may get different metaphors or downloads that differ from one client to the other.

Depending on how this ability manifests itself, different psychics use them for different purposes. Believe it or not, some people use their clairvoyant abilities to find lost items. It is not uncommon that you find a psychic with heightened visionary senses to help others find their keys, pets, etc. This gift does not only help their bearers grasp a deeper understanding of their souls and the souls of the entire universe, but they can also use it for the better good.

Clairaudience

Clairaudience refers to the ability to receive audible messages from a higher entity or the spiritual world. Those with clairaudient abilities can hear sounds that no one else can hear, surpassing the normal level of consciousness and the physical world. You must be incredibly intuitive to receive vocal messages from the spiritual realm.

The messages received may be very clear, meaning that the psychic may receive certain words or phrases or hear specific names, or they may be vague with music or other undiscernible sounds. The sounds often differ from what we usually hear in the physical world. Psychics may feel like the words are being spoken directly into their ears or inside their heads. They may also hear noises that echo from a different realm. They are usually tormenting and rather harsh. The sounds remain constant, with a calm, even tone. Some psychics hear the voices of their loved ones who have passed. Clairaudients usually receive their messages during significant times, such as emergencies or crises. The voices also make themselves heard to guide the psychic when they are at a crossroads for guidance. Some psychics hear the voices of spirits in their dreams. Most psychic downloads that are intended for clients are straightforward and short.

Many of those who have clairaudient abilities seldom realize it or speak of it. This is because hearing sounds that no one else can hear is a symptom of schizophrenia or psychosis. Even those who know all about clairaudience and are aware of their abilities may struggle to make sense of the messages they receive, especially when they are not straightforward or are just random sounds.

Clairsentience

Clairsentience messages are purely felt, making them the most common intuitive ability among these four clairs. Everyone has gut instincts, regardless of how strong or otherwise they are felt. Many people are also empathetic, which gives them the ability to sense other people's emotions or feel the overall vibe of a room. Clairsentient psychics can tell the energy of others as soon as they see them or start talking to them. While this is a significant intuitive ability, it can add a lot to reading when combined with other psychic abilities. Whenever a psychic receives a message, their clairsentience usually lets them know how important the information is for their client.

Those with high clairsentient abilities have access to the energies and feelings of people. They also sense the energies attached to certain objects, places, or events. They can easily relate to everything happening in front of them and the things that occur at different times and places. Their heightened intuition and empathy give them access to psychic-level information. This means they just "know" stuff with no logic or reason attached. Clairsentients know and feel things that have not been previously disclosed to them. While we can all get a feel for certain vibes or energies, clairsentients experience more intense feelings that can not be ignored. This intensity and pronounced clarity give them access to more information than the average empathetic person can obtain.

Clairsentients are easily drawn to strong vibrational energies, whether they are positive or negative. This is why they can tend to take things very personally and are likely to be burdened by the unhelpful emotions and experiences of others. This is also why they must always cleanse their energy fields and indulge in self-care practices.

If a clairsentient gives a person with physical ailments a reading, they will more than likely feel their client's condition in their own body. For instance, if someone is struggling with digestive issues, the psychic may feel tingling, or any other sensation, in their belly. If the client, or someone close to them, is experiencing knee joint pain, they will feel an ache in that area.

Claircognizance

Claircognizance is often confused with clairsentience because of how similar the abilities are. Like clairsentients, claircognizants just know things without proper logical reasoning. They just know the reality of things or can tell when things are about to happen, even though there are no signs indicating that. If you speak to a claircognizant psychic, they will be able to tell that you grew up with a narcissistic mother or just got out of a toxic relationship. Claircognizants can even tell that you struggle with your highly sensitive child because of how cautious you need to be around them. They do that by sharpening their intuition, surrounding subconscious obstructions, traumas, unhealed wounds, and past pains. They can tell exactly what is holding you back, and through that, they can reveal what kind of relationship patterns or complex connections you have in your life.

A claircognizant's intuition offers them an instant, large download of their client's struggles and life situation. Like clairsentient, they are encountered with a prominent gut feeling that they can not shake away, no matter how hard they try. The difference here is that the psychic download manifests as thoughts instead of sensing the energy or "feeling" the information.

For many claircognizants, their messages come through as light bulbs that light up inside the head. This phenomenon usually lasts for a flash of a second. Psychics can receive these intuitive news flashes at any time, whether working, watching television, working out, or painting. While you would expect them to be involved in an activity that is somewhat related to the information received, considering that they come in as thoughts, this is rarely the case.

Claircognizant abilities can be burdensome for many people, especially since they often warn them about the people they know and care about. After all, it is never good to learn that one of your closest friends has been lying to you. Nevertheless, even though there are some things that you think you are better off not knowing about, this ability can give you indispensable insights and knowledge. It can help guide you in numerous areas of your life.

Developing Psychic Abilities

It does not matter where you currently stand in your psychic journey or what your beliefs regarding psychics are because the chances are that you have your own intuitive psychic tendencies. Most spiritual and psychic individuals believe that we all have extraordinary inclinations. All we need to do is learn how to develop and refine them.

The words intuitive and psychic are almost synonymous. Being highly intuitive allows you to tap into your inner powers. When you achieve a high enough level of consciousness, you'll be able to feel, think, see, or hear things far beyond our physical world. Many people already unknowingly experience this phenomenon daily.

Intuition is perhaps the only gift that everyone in the world possesses. If you think about it, qualities and traits are only described as gifts when only a portion of the world has them, except for intuition. Everyone has it, but only a few people recognize its power and capitalize on it.

Refining Your Clairvoyance

1. Meditate

To develop your clairvoyant abilities, get in a comfortable position and breathe deeply and evenly. Make sure your breathing is rhythmic before shifting focus to your third eye chakra. Imagine that you are breathing light through this energy center throughout the entire meditation practice. Stay in this meditative state for as long as you desire and practice it regularly.

2. Gaze at the Sun

While this seems like a painful practice, it can significantly raise your vibrations and clear the clairvoyant communication pathways. Face the direction of the sun, directing your third eye toward it. Make sure to wear sunscreen and close your eyes! Moonlight gazing is also effective.

3. Activate Your Third Eye Chakra

Meditation, introspection, crystals such as amethyst, labradorite, sodalite, and yoga are just a few things that can help you activate your third eye chakra.

4. Improve Your Diet

Eat a balanced and healthy diet and focus on foods such as mushrooms, noni juice, and honey that help you support your third eye chakra.

5. Use Vibrations

Vibrate your third eye chakra by singing, chanting, humming, or using a singing bowl. This can help you clear any obstructions and stubborn energies, ensuring a free flow in your psychic communication channels.

6. Use Crystals and Essential Oils

Use selenite, clear quartz, lapis-lazuli, amethyst, or other third eye chakra crystals in your meditative practice. Place it on your forehead for the best results. You can also place the crystal on the mat as you practice yoga. Rubbing essential oils like rosemary, palo santo, frankincense, and lavender on your forehead is also highly effective.

Developing Clairaudience

1. Meditate

Get in a comfortable position before inhaling, filling your entire abdomen with air. Then, exhale forcefully. Do this a few times while keeping your consciousness within the physical frame of your being. Imagine that golden light is clearing the space around your ears and temples.

2. Clear Your Throat Chakra

Singing, chanting, and humming can help you clear your throat chakra. You should also avoid negative conversations and gossip.

3. Use Crystals

Hold healing stones like sodalite, selenite, and labradorite around your ears and temples. You can wear throat chakra crystals as earrings or necklaces if you wish. They can also be incorporated into your meditative and yoga practice.

4. Practice Active Listening

Sit down and breathe steadily and deeply. Keep your thoughts and emotions at bay as you focus on your surroundings. Listen to all the sounds around you, whether it is the wind, the running car engine in the street, the birds, or a panting dog.

Strengthening Your Clairsentience

1. Use Crystals

Hold crystals like rose quartz or unakite jasper close to your heart. As with other crystals, you can meditate with it or do yoga in its presence. You can also wear it as a pendant on a long necklace.

2. Create a Safe Space

Create a clutter-free space in your home that you can retreat to whenever you feel overwhelmed by external energies and emotions. You can also use this space to practice heart chakra-specific meditations and yoga poses.

3. Try Smudging

Use palo santo or sage to smudge your home and body to ground your aura.

Achieving Claircognizance

1. Practice Automatic Writing

You can either use an electronic device or pen and paper for this practice. Write down everything that comes to mind, regardless of how stupid it seems to be. Let your subconscious mind take the lead, allowing your consciousness to just watch.

2. Use Crystals

Using solar plexus chakra-specific crystals can help you clear your claircognizant communication pathways. These include citrine, tiger's eye, pyrite, amber, and golden apatite.

3. Meditation

Practicing any type of meditation for at least five minutes a day can help you heighten your intuitive senses. Over time, you'll be able to quiet your thoughts and tune into your intuition.

How often do you suddenly turn around because you can feel someone's eyes on you? Have you ever thought of someone just to find them ringing you up later in the day? Perhaps you have got the chills upon entering a room or had a bad feeling about a trip that ended up horrendous. These are not coincidences. They are your psychic gifts trying to tell you something. The first step toward developing your psychic abilities is learning to trust your intuition. It is there for a reason!

Chapter 7: Psychic Reiki Practicum 1 - Healing Yourself

Reiki energy can be a wonderful source of restorative power even Level one practitioners can apply. At this level, practitioners first learn how to heal themselves using their Reiki skills of energy manipulation and intuition. Later on, you'll also master how to use the same techniques to help others heal. This chapter is dedicated to teaching you self-healing methods to empower yourself when recuperating from a medical condition or injury. Helping others will be discussed in the following chapter. With its beginner-friendly exercises and comprehensive explanations, the techniques in this chapter will provide the perfect foundation for a new and healthier life.

Preparing Your Environment

Although Reiki is a universal life force within you, you must create an environment free of distractions and negative spiritual influences to enhance it with natural psychic energy. Make sure to find a place where you can stay safe, comfortable, and focused during your sessions. Unless you suffer from a medical condition that requires round-the-clock care, it is also recommended you perform the self-healing exercises alone. The beauty of Reiki's hand-healing techniques lies in their simplicity. Because they are so simple, they can be done in any position you feel comfortable with as long as you are in an environment where you can relax.

Try using it regularly once you find a space that fits all these requirements. It is fine to make changes when traveling, but try not to switch it around too much. In addition, if you feel more focused without any distracting noises, feel free to work in complete silence. That way, you can focus only on the sounds of your body and develop a deeper connection with your intuition. However, many practitioners prefer listening to relaxing music before and even during their Reiki sessions.

Activating Your Hands

Before you start practicing any Reiki healing technique, the first thing to learn is how to make your hand receptive to psychic energy. This involves sensing it with your hands and drawing it toward your palms. While Masters often ignore this step, beginner practitioners can not afford to do the same. Unlike them, you are just developing your connection with Reiki energy, and without the proper connection, you'll not have anything to use in the healing session.

The benefits of activating your hands include:

- Drawing more energy into your hands
- Symbol activation becomes easier
- You are showing respect to the energy, symbols, and your guides
- You are activating your chakras, the most energy-sensitive points of your body

There are several ways to activate your hands. Here is a simple way to do it:

- Sit or stand in a relaxed position and close your eyes.
- Take a deep breath, then exhale. Repeat until you feel your body and mind calming down.
- With your palms pointing forward, elevate your hands above your head. You can draw a symbol, hold a trinket in your hand or even call upon your spiritual guide during this process.
- Visualize the psychic energy above your head and see it entering through your crown chakra.

- Allow the energy to flow through your body until it reaches your hands.
- When you feel completely energized, you'll be ready to use Reiki.

Establishing a Deeper Connection

Having activated your hands, you'll feel confident and encouraged to do great things with your newfound power. However, you must remember that one or even a handful of successful connections does not guarantee that the Reiki energy will stay with you forever.

Here are a few tips to deepen this connection, so you can call on your intuitive power whenever you need it:

- Start your days with a quick session. 15-30 minutes of hands-on Reiki practice every morning after waking up will allow you to stay grounded through your day.
- Implement daily gratitude. Practice saying thanks for the energy and the help of symbols and spiritual guides aiding you during your session daily.
- Finish your day with Reiki. Repeat your morning technique before going to bed to have a restful sleep.
- Kill spare time with Reiki. Whether you are waiting in line in the grocery store, waiting for friends to arrive at a restaurant, or traveling on public transport, it is the ideal time for grounding Reiki exercises.
- Practice hand activation. Make the conscious decision to practice receiving Reiki energy through your palms as frequently as possible.
- Practice at your own pace. Feel free to take your time with the exercises, and do not worry about not practicing enough. Everyone has their own way of connecting to their intuition, so you know best what works for you.

Self-Healing Reiki Hand Movements

While it is good to have a dedicated time for your session, with an area established for practicing, you can do a session whenever you feel the need for it. You will simply go to this dedicated place, get comfortable, and relax with your preferred method. This can be music, breathing in silence, calling on spiritual guides, etc. Remove your shoes and go through the hand-activating or empowering step. If you lie down, place a pillow under your head and maybe a small blanket to cover your body. If not, just stay or sit in a comfortable position with your shoulders relaxed and slightly rolled back.

Close your eyes and proceed with scanning your body for areas that need healing. When you have identified the problematic areas, you can try to relax a little bit more by focusing on your breaths. This will also help you focus on performing the hand positions by employing all your energy. There are several different hand positions that you can apply during a self-healing process. Each of them is designed to assist in relieving the symptoms in a particular area of your body. While their description below should give you a great head start on how each of them should be performed, it is recommended that you focus on the areas where you have found issues while scanning.

Each hand movement should be applied for no more than 5 minutes at each session. It is better to repeat the exercises several times a day to ensure positive energy flow towards the desired areas than to swamp them with an overflow of energy all at once, as this can slow down the healing process. Below are the hand positions you can use for Reiki healing.

Face

Face position.
https://pxhere.com/en/photo/1616861

One of the first positions in Reiki's hand placement is the face position. It works for the issue associated with the throat and third eye chakras.

- Take a deep breath and raise your hands to your face
- Rest your palms against your face by covering your eyes and forehead
- Keep your hands there for the allocated time without applying any pressure

Crown

This position addresses issues in your crown chakra, alleviating headaches and other symptoms related to this region.

- Place your hands on either side of your head, palms resting above your ears and below the top of your head
- Take a deep breath and feel the energy coursing through your fingertips near your crown
- Keep breathing in and out and holding your head for four to five minutes or until you feel your symptoms dissipate

Back of the Head

As in the previous exercise, this hand position is also geared towards the head and spine-related symptoms and realigning the course of energy through your body.

- Close your eyes and cross your arms behind your head
- Put one hand just above the nape of your neck and the other one on the back of the head
- Inhale and let the energy flow through your body until you exhale
- Repeat for two to three minutes before opening your eyes

Jawline

This position aligns energy in your jawline and chin areas, alleviating symptoms in facial muscles, teeth, and gums.

- Cup your jawline with your hands, palms resting on your chin
- Secure your hold but do not put too much pressure on your jaw
- Inhale and exhale several times until you feel your jaw relaxing and the tension leaving this area

Chest

This is another great way to start your session, especially if you are working on several different areas and require the assistance of your spiritual guides.

Chest position.
https://pixabay.com/es/photos/ni%c3%b1a-orando-las-manos-rezar-ojo-20878/

- Join your hands in a prayer position in front of your chest. They should be joined just below your chin, a little higher than when reciting a prayer.
- Keep your hand joined while concentrating on your breathing for three to five minutes. Not exerting too much pressure with your hands will help you stay focused.
- Release the air from your lungs and lower your hands to your sides.
- Continue breathing in and out until you feel ready to either move on to the next hand placement or perform a post-treatment scan.

Shoulder Blades

The shoulders are crucial in supporting your body and the energetic flow through it. This hand placement will help restore this function.

- Put your hands flat on your shoulders, keeping your elbows bent. Then, raise your hands up over your head.
- If you can not reach it from behind, you can also place your hands on your shoulders from the front of your body. Your shoulders and hands should remain relaxed.
- Close your eyes and take deep breaths until you feel the tension dissipating

Neck, Collarbone, and Heart

The space between your neck and your heart is one of the most significant regions of your energetic systems, with numerous issues related to it.

- Form a V-shape with the thumb and the fingers of your non-dominant hand
- Place this hand on your neck, slightly cupping it
- Put your other hand between your heart and your collarbone
- Hold the position while breathing deeply for four to five minutes

Rib Cage

This hand placement heals the symptoms originating from your rib cage, which is essentially the pathway between your heart and solar plexus centers.

- Close your eyes and place one of your hands on the lower end of your breastbone
- Place the other hand slightly below the first one
- Inhale and relax your elbows to allow the energy to flow from your hands towards your rib cage
- Hold the position for two to three minutes

Abdominal Area

This hand placement is for healing digestion-related conditions and issues with endocrine glands located in your abdomen.

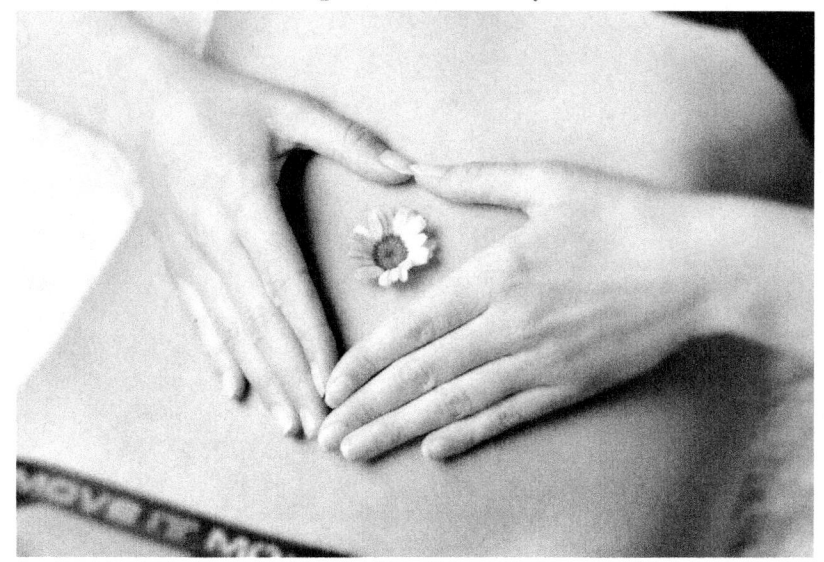

Abdominal position.
https://pixabay.com/es/photos/mujer-barriga-dolor-de-est%c3%b3mago-3186730/

- Put your hands on your stomach, just above your navel
- Make sure your fingers are touching at the tips but not interlaced
- Relax your elbows and breath in and out for a few minutes

The Middle of Your Back

Placing your hands on the middle of your back supports your spine, reinforcing your resolution to combat your condition.

- With your elbows bent, move your hands behind your back
- Place your hands on your mid-back area and take a deep breath
- Hold the position for one or two minutes or until it feels comfortable to you

Lower Back

Hand placement on the lower back is beneficial for your entire energetic system as this area can be affected by myriad conditions.

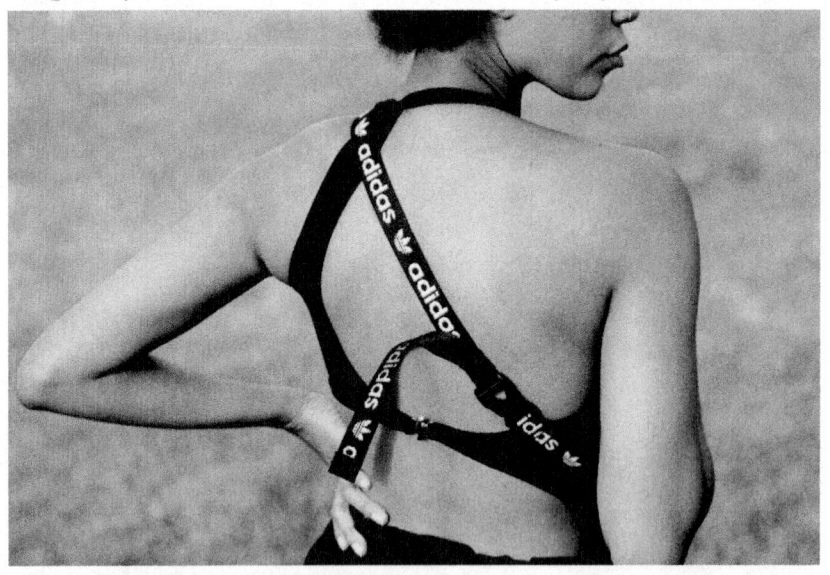

Lower back position.
https://www.pexels.com/photo/woman-in-black-sports-bra-3621646/

- Start by reaching behind your back and putting your palms on your lower back. This is just below your rib cage, where your kidneys are.
- Make sure that your elbows are bent. If not, adjust the position until they are.
- Hold the position for the maximum allocated time, then release it with an exhale.

Pelvic Area

By placing your hands on your pelvic bones, you can ensure they provide sufficient protection for the organs they encapsulate.

- Place your hands on your pelvic bones, fingers pointing towards the middle of your pelvic region
- As with the rib cage placement, your fingertips should touch in the middle
- Breathe in and out for two to three minutes or until you feel your pelvic area relaxing

Sacrum

This hand placement is designed to relax the muscles in your sacral area and allow any illness related to this region to heal naturally.

- Take a deep breath and place your harm on your sacrum below your waist and kidneys
- Exhale and focus on sensing how your muscles and nerves relax in this area of your body
- Continue holding the pose for three to five minutes while breathing in and out deeply

Legs

If you have any root chakra or other grounding issues, this hand placement technique will help overcome them.

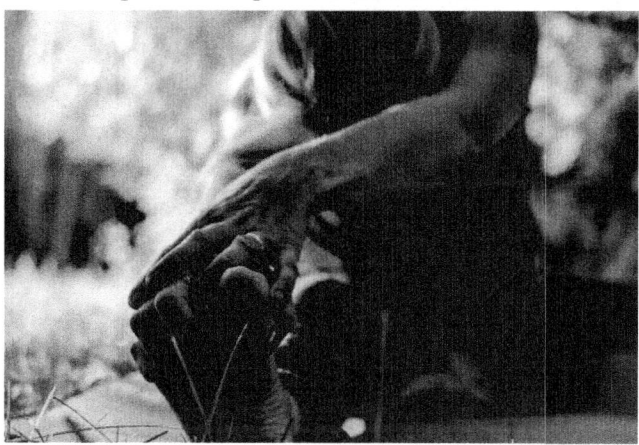

Leg position.
https://pixabay.com/es/photos/yoga-calma-liberar-extensi%c3%b3n-2662234/

- Start in a sitting position with your hands extended towards your legs
- Lean forward so that you can touch the soles of your feet. Do this one foot at a time
- If you can not reach the soles of your feet, you can place one of your hands on the top of your foot
- Crossing one leg over the other knee will help you reach both of your feet without having to twist your back to the side or strain your entire body unnecessarily
- Hold your hand on one of your feet for one to two minutes, then switch to the other one

Tips for Finding the Problematic Areas

As established early on in this book, Psychic Reiki is a highly intuitive practice. Not only do you need to use your instincts to sense the energy, but you must also channel it telepathically through your body. Any technique, including the hand positions presented in this practicum, is subject to individual interpretation. While they can be used as they are, their effects can be significantly heightened by putting your own interpretation on them.

You may wonder how you can intuitively scan your body and sense blockages. One of the most commonly used techniques for this purpose is called Byosen Reikan-ho. This self-scanning method, which involves feeling the resonance of a hand position, was taught by Usui himself. Before Byosen Reikan-ho is applied, you must activate your hands using your intuition, symbols, spiritual guides, and whatever aids you have chosen to employ. You may also want to clean the space and start scanning your body, starting from your head. Since the purpose of the scan is to reveal areas needing more attention, it is critical to be as receptive to the change in energy as you can during this process. The best way to find out if you are at the right place is to move your hand several times over the body part you sense the fluctuation taking place.

The latter can be used for any other technique you use for scanning, as well as Byosen Reikan-ho. Whichever scanning method you choose, make sure to repeat it before and after the healing session. This way, you can ensure that the treatment was completed successfully and evaluate whether it's working.

Disclaimer

It is important to note that Reiki energy should only be considered an empowerment tool for your healing journey and not an actual healing technique. If you suffer from any condition or injury, seek medical assistance for it first. After establishing the proper course of treatment with the help of a medical professional, you can consult them about alternative aids, such as Reiki. If they approve this method, you may use it to facilitate your healing experience and maintain your health after regaining it. Remember that while Reiki is a gentle healing technique, it is not appropriate for every illness. For example, Reiki energy can cause broken bones to heal very quickly. This could be a problem if the bones are not set properly. In this case, the doctor will not recommend Reiki until the bones are set and are at least partially healed. Reiki should not be used on active infections either, as it can heighten the discomfort.

Chapter 8: Psychic Reiki Practicum 2 - Healing Others

Once you have learned how to use Reiki healing techniques on yourself, you can move on to deepen your sense of intuition. This helps you to transfer your positive physic energy to others and support them in their healing journey. While you can start using hand placement techniques on others as a Level one practitioner, you'll learn more advanced techniques at Level two of your training. Apart from these advanced methods, the traditional Reiki symbols are also revealed in Level two, giving you a further tool for manipulating psychic energy. This chapter will explain several essential symbols and deal with practical advice for growing your intuition. We will also mention some advanced healing techniques that Reiki Masters have traditionally taught. Even if you are not ready to look into the advanced techniques, you can still combine the symbols with the blockage-sensing and simple hand placement methods mentioned in the previous chapter.

Improving Your Intuition

While intuition is something everyone is born with, as you have read in the previous chapter, there are plenty of ways to intensify it. Tapping into your intuitive powers is a prerequisite for healing yourself and others. If you want to move on from healing yourself to channeling your psychic energy to heal others, you must strengthen your intuition. Not only that, but sensing blockages in a body will require advanced, intuitive ability. You can use the Byosen Reikanho technique to improve your scanning abilities or look into other methods for the same purpose. You do not even have to use them as they are. As you do the entire scanning, sensing, and healing session, you can put a twist on any technique designed to build up your intuition. Remember, the power comes from within you, and the only way to get it out is by using the method that suits you.

You can practice enhancing your intuitive powers by yourself, or better yet, on another person. Of course, practicing with someone you know well is different from working with someone you can only get to know through intuition, but it will give you a head start, nevertheless. Ask them not to reveal anything about what they are feeling, then simply close your eyes and start focusing on your senses. Notice anything you feel, hear, or see; even close your eyes. The stimuli will unveil what your gut is telling you about the condition of the person in front of you. After repeating this several times, your ability to notice even the minor changes in someone's body will be heightened, and you'll be able to recall this power without even trying.

If you have trouble channeling your intuition to sense energy changes in others, you can ask your spiritual guides to help you out. You may not receive or have the ability to interpret the advice during the same practice session in which you made your request, but you'll certainly find it useful later on. Again, repetition is the key to successfully fine-tuning your intuitive abilities with the help of a higher spirit.

Sometimes you just have to look into what your gut is telling you and simply go with it. Ask a friend or family member to send you a photo of someone unknown to you. After contemplating every bit of information, you can intuitively gather about the unknown person and ask them to verify this information. Note everything you have gotten right, and try to call back the sensations you had when you received this information. You want to focus on these sensations next time you want to work on your intuitive powers.

Reiki Symbols

Reiki symbols are passed down by master's teaching Level two Reiki and onwards. Each sign works with specific characteristics that will help you channel psychic energy. However, the use of symbols is entirely up to the practitioner. Feel free to try them, but if you feel your intuition is enough to guide you through the healing session, you can omit using symbols. This may vary depending on your mental, physical, and spiritual state and the condition of your subject. Sometimes you'll not feel the need to reach for symbols at all. Whereas at other times, you'll be prompted to call on them for added reinforcement.

Types of Reiki Symbols

The main reason Reiki symbols are only revealed at Level two is that you must pass a certain spiritual threshold before you can call on them and harness their powers. And even then, it takes further spiritual growth before you can access all the symbols. Like crystals, symbols also differ in their vibration, which means that you'll need different symbols for awareness, healing, and achieving higher levels of consciousness.

Here is the list of benefits you can gain through different symbols:

- Balancing and aligning chakras and chakra systems
- Channeling Reiki into a problematic area
- Physical, mental, and spiritual healing,
- Clearing out blockages from chakras
- Attracting positive psychic energy
- Connecting with your spiritual guides
- Grounding yourself and others in the present
- Providing abundance in whatever you or others desire

Below are some Reiki symbols you can use in your practice. They can be applied as they are or modified to suit your purposes better. Not only that, but you can design your own symbols and use them. Nothing helps more with channeling intuitive power than the symbols created after an intrinsic vision.

Cho Ku Rei

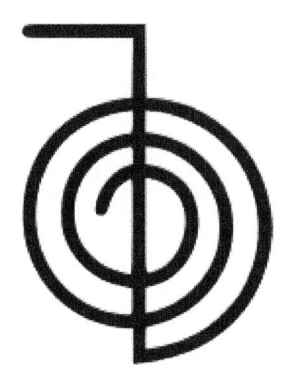

Cho Ku Rei symbol.
Chokurei.jpg: Stephen Buck The Reiki Sanghaderivative work: LeonardoelRojo, CC BY-SA 2.0 <https://creativecommons.org/licenses/by-sa/2.0>, via Wikimedia Commons https://commons.wikimedia.org/wiki/File:Chokurei.svg:

Also known as the Power symbol, Cho Ku Rei is a tool for changing the energy intensity in a particular chakra or body part. It allows you to transfer energy between your body and the body of the person you are healing. This symbol is represented as a coil, which you can use to increase or decrease power, depending on which direction you are drawing it. Cho Ku Rei is activated by visualizing a switch next to the symbol. Once activated, it will increase your ability to channel Reiki through your body and guide you through your session.

Sei He Ki

Sei He Ki symbol.
Stephen Buck The Reiki Sangha, CC BY-SA 4.0 <https://creativecommons.org/licenses/by-sa/4.0>, via Wikimedia Commons https://commons.wikimedia.org/wiki/File:Seiheiki.jpg:

Sei He Ki, or the Harmony symbol, is particularly good for mental clarity and emotional balance. Its name can be translated as "God and man become one," and it is often illustrated as either a bird's outstretched wings or a wave looming over a beach. This is a great symbol for promoting balance in the mind, bringing the two sides of a person together. It can also be used to ward off an imbalance.

Hon Sha Ze Sho Nen

Symbol of distance.
Stephen Buck The Reiki Sangha, CC BY-SA 4.0 <https://creativecommons.org/licenses/by-sa/4.0>, via Wikimedia Commons https://commons.wikimedia.org/wiki/File:Honshazeshonen.jpg:

The symbol of distance is often used for healing at a distance. It is a more complex symbol and is usually taught on higher levels. The direct translation talks about having no past, present, or future, speaking about reiki healing over long distances. For example, you can send Reiki through the symbol into someone's past and modify their experience by putting things into a different perspective. This will help them heal from past traumas and move on with their lives. You can also use the symbol to send energy into the future to prepare someone for a negative experience.

Shika Sei Ki Reiki

Shika Sei Ki Reiki's vibrations resonate with the heart chakra's energy and are used to treat any issues related to this center. It helps remove negative influences from the heart chakra, allowing the vital life force to flow through it once again. This eliminates negative emotions and thought patterns, revitalizing a person's mind, body, and soul.

Nin Giz Zida

This symbol is used for spiritual cleansing and is known as the serpent of fire. It channels energy through all the chakras, aligning them or balancing their functions. You can use it to relax your mind and body before a session or to bring the person you are working on into a state of serenity. Nin Giz Zida is often combined with other symbols for grounding, focusing intention, clearing energetic paths, and other purposes.

Shika So Reiki

Typically taught at Usui level two, Shika So Reiki is a symbol used to alleviate symptoms related to throat chakra blockages and malfunctions. This symbol can heal thyroid imbalances or other issues with boy regulation. On a wider scale, it can aid imbalances in a society or group.

The Dragon of Fire

The Dragon of Fire symbol can help form a connection with nature's psychic energy and balance the flow of different forms of power. Sometimes, a person's issues stem from a drastic difference in their vibrations and the vibrational energy of the universal life force around them. This symbol can help you realign the person's energy by challenging natural energy into them. It can also serve as a shield against negative energy when activated in front of the body.

How Reiki Symbols Work and How to Activate Them

Reiki symbols are carriers for the energy you harness from the spiritual world. Each sign is linked to several forms of energy and spiritual guides that emit healing vibrations. As a result, Reiki symbols can boost your psychic energy levels, healing your mind, body, and spirit during the process. When conducting energy through your body, you are doing this through intent. When you include symbols in your intention, your ability to channel the universal life force is magnified. They boost your vibration, allowing the energy to flow more freely and rapidly. This helps you uncover the root of chakra imbalances and blockages in your body and in the body of others, after which you can find the best way to heal them.

Before you can use any of the symbols, you must activate them with Reiki energy. There are a few ways to do this:

- **Drawing:** You can draw symbols on chakras, talismans, or wherever you may feel you can use them. If you are going to draw a symbol before a scan or treatment session, trace its outline with your index, thumb, index, and middle fingers joined together. This will concentrate the energy, making it easier to channel wherever you need it to travel.
- **Visualizing:** Symbols you use regularly will be engraved in your brain, which means you can simply envision using them. Just set your intention towards a symbol you know the benefits of, and it will soon be at your service.
- **Chanting Their Name:** If you have trouble visualizing a symbol, chant their name three times, and they will appear in the physical world.

Planting Symbols into a Person's Energy Field

This is one of the most common ways to use symbols in your practice. It is very subtle yet powerful, making it perfect for beginners needing a major boost when learning their trade. You may initially struggle with emotional blocks or unwanted thoughts during your healing sessions. Even if you learn how to dismiss these from your own thoughts, you may find them way harder to deal with in someone else's body and mind. By placing empowering symbols into their energy field, you can keep the distracting thought patterns at bay even after the session.

The planting technique is particularly beneficial in cases when you can not apply hand placement techniques due to specific injuries or conditions. It is easier to use than distance healing but will have the same powerful effect. Typically, it is applied through the crown chakra as this is the best way to channel Reiki through someone. This works on the same principle as when you are receiving empowering energy when you are preparing yourself for healing.

Traditional Reiki Techniques

As mentioned earlier, traditional Reiki approaches are only taught by masters on all levels. Here are a few examples of the techniques you can learn as a Reiki practitioner:

- **Gassho Meiso:** A meditation technique to help you focus your mind and energy during a healing session
- **Joshin Kokyu-Ho:** Breathing exercise that strengthens and cleanses your spirit
- **Kenyoku:** Also called dry bathing, it helps you leave all distractions behind and ground you to the present
- **Reiki Mawashi:** A group exercise that allows several practitioners to share their psychic energy, empowering each other in the process
- **Nats -Ho:** Another detoxification technique for your mind, body, and soul

- **Enkaku Chiryo:** Also known as Shashin Chiryo, a distance healing technique that teaches how to make associations through photographs, names, etc.
- **Gyoshi-Ho and Koki-Ho:** The first one teaches healing with eyes, the second with the breath (they are always taught together)
- **Seiheki Chiryo:** This allows you to heal unhealthy habits and addictive behavior by transforming them into healthy ones
- **Nentatsu-Ho:** Used to deprogram someone's mind to remove unwanted through processes
- **Jacki-Kiri Joka-Ho:** This technique teaches how to transform negative energy present in an object into positive energy you can use for reinforcement
- **Byogen Chiryo:** Helps reveal and treat the origin of certain conditions, mainly mental ones
- **Tanden Chiryo:** A psychic power-up tool for yourself or the person you want to heal

If you have trouble determining which technique to use on others, you can use the ***Reiji-ho technique*** to guide you. Its name is translated as the indication of the spirit, which means you'll receive assistance from the Spirit of Reiki. Essentially, this is another way to enhance your intuition when scanning someone's energy field for possible issues. Apart from the technique itself, Reiji-ho can also reveal the symbols and hand placements you should use during your session. Depending on the malady you are dealing with and your experience level, you may also need to use Reiji-ho during the session. Feel free to use it anytime you need guidance, even if you have already used certain treatments for specific conditions. Remember, each person has a unique constitution and energetic field. A treatment that works for one person may not work for another person with the same condition. This is exactly why you need to rely on your intuition.

Disclaimer

Once again, you are reminded that while Psychic Reiki is a valuable power enhancement tool, it is not an officially recognized healing technique. This is even more critical to emphasize when you have others that rely on your help on their healing journey. Advise them that if they suffer from any condition or injury, they should seek medical assistance for it first. After establishing the proper course of treatment with the help of a medical professional and getting their approval for alternative aids, such as Reiki, your client can turn to you for Reiki healing sessions. Certain conditions cannot be treated with psychic healing, regardless of how mild the method you are using. Other times, the medical professional will advise against certain techniques such as direct hand placement but approve distance healing, or vice versa.

People with an active infection or undergoing cancer treatment should not be treated with Reiki. Firstly, while the healing energy can remove the toxins, it could help spread them, aggravating the condition. Secondly, the toxins are part of the treatment and should not be removed from the body. As the frequency of energetic vibrations may trigger seizures or disrupt the work of pacemakers, people who have epilepsy or who have pacemakers should not be treated with Reiki healing.

Chapter 9: Psychic Reiki Practicum 3 - Psychic Distance Healing

All the intuition-boosting techniques you were introduced to in the previous two chapters can be a stepping stone to more advanced healing techniques for yourself and others. They can also become a tool to prepare your body and mind to hone your telepathic abilities and venture into distance healing. This chapter discusses this unique form of healing, which allows you to alleviate symptoms without being in the same room as the person you are treating. You will learn how this technique works in the traditional system and how you can use your psychic powers to personalize the method. This will allow you to find the therapy suitable for you and the person you are treating, and you'll be more effective.

How Distance Healing Works

After learning about the benefits of hand placement techniques and healing through energy transfer in one-on-one and group sessions, you may wonder how Reiki works at a distance. Is energy not weakened when sent through a greater distance? And if it is, what is the purpose of sending it to someone who needs empowerment? The answer to these questions is not that clear-cut. Traditional energetic waves are prone to fatigue when crossing great distances, but the ones you create in your brain when using your psychic abilities are not. This is why you can send Reiki telepathically across space and time. If someone across the world needs a boost of energy to deal with physical and mental conditions, you can send it to them through distance healing techniques.

Healing from the Past

While you cannot change anyone's past, you can put their experiences into a different perspective through Reiki healing. Traumatic experiences from the past often lead to chakra imbalances in the present. In fact, it is more common for people with emotional trauma to seek Reiki treatment than people suffering from other conditions. When someone's past affects their present life, it can be easily picked up during the initial session, even if they do not talk about it beforehand. People often can not help but think about the trauma during the session, even when asked to relax. You will definitely sense this when you connect to them telepathically. Fortunately, you can bring painful memories to the surface and envelop them in positive energy. This changes the patterns around them, so the recipient can move on with their life.

Healing in the Present

Healing in the present time is particularly useful for critical situations, such as when someone needs your help immediately, and they cannot get to you. In this case, you can send a high amount of positive energy as soon as you are notified of the situation. However, things do not need to be urgent to send Reiki in the present, and it is sometimes simply more convenient to do it this way.

Healing in the Future

While it is far less common, distance healing is also used to send Reiki into the future. If someone has an upcoming event, appointment, or interview they feel anxious about, energy sent ahead of time can calm their nerves and help them get through the situation confidently. Even knowing they will be able to rely on this little boost when the time comes can reduce their stress and keep their health and happiness balanced.

Preparatory Steps for Distance Healing

Depending on individual circumstances, distance healing can be initiated in several different ways. Regardless of the method you choose, there are several steps you should follow. First and foremost, you should always inform the person about your intent and get their consent before actually sending the restorative energy life force. Make sure to share as many details about the transfer as possible so they can prepare themselves to receive the power boost. This should include the exact date and time you'll send the energy and instructions on what they should or should not do during the transfer.

When you tell a person about your intent, encourage them to discuss what they hope to achieve with the treatment. Ask them about the state of their health and whether their doctor approves of Reiki as an alternative treatment if they have a health condition. Once everything is clear on both sides, you can remind them when you'll be sending energy. You may also call or message them before you start channeling Reiki. This is an optional step to ensure they are in a stress-free environment where they will not be distracted by anything or anyone.

Essentially, all your client needs to do when receiving Reiki from a distance is to sit down or lie back and relax. Ideally, they should be in their homes to receive it, but they can choose to do it at their workplace during lunch. As long as they stay still during the transfer, they can pick the best time and place that suits them. The transfer can last from 10 minutes to an hour, depending on how much boost they need.

Using the Reiki Distance-Healing Symbol

When it comes to sending Reiki, every Reiki Practitioner has their own preferences. Their approach often depends on what the recipient wants to achieve. The most commonly used method uses the distant healing symbol, Hon-Sha-Ze-Sho-Nen, combined with one or more other empowering symbols like Cho Ku Rei and Sei-He Ki.

Cho Ku Rei, the power symbol, is often used in distance healing in a traditional sequence called the Reiki Sandwich. While the sequence can be used for other purposes, in this case, it consists of two power symbols and the distance healing symbol in the middle. Here is how to do this method:

- Write the recipient's name and the purpose of the treatment on a piece of paper. Fold it and keep it in your hands, palms facing each other.
- Let your body relax and allow your eyes to close.
- Repeat what's written on the paper, visualize Cho Ku Rei, and connect to the energy of the symbol.
- Now switch your intent towards Hon-Sha-Ze-Sho-Nen and visualize it beside or on top of Cho Ku Rei.
- Follow up with another Cho Ku Rei, which you can place on top or on the other side of Hon-Sha-Ze-Sho-Nen.
- Now, Hon-Sha-Ze-Sho-Nen is empowered on both sides, and you'll be able to see where to use it in your client's chakra system.
- You can start transferring the sequence into the recipient's mind along with the boost of a positive life force.
- When sending Reiki, do not try to channel it towards a specific area. The highest interest of the receiver is to get empowered mentally, so they can deal with their issues, whether physical or mental.
- Visualize the energy enveloping your client and soak in every detail of your experience as you may want to share it with them in the future.

When the transfer has been completed, let the client digest the new sensation for a few minutes or hours. Later on, you can ask them about their experience. If they describe feeling more relaxed than before, the new vital force is now taking effect in their body. Depending on their goals, some clients may experience an emotional release or have visions of certain activities, objects, or events.

If they had a visual experience, you could compare it to yours and see if there were any similarities between what you both saw. This will help you develop your telepathic abilities even more. Not only that, but if clients need any additional help, you'll be able to connect to them even faster.

Other Ways to Channel Energy

Apart from the traditional distance healing technique, there are several other ways to connect with the person you are trying to heal. Ideally, the connection should be made telepathically as this is the best way to transfer energy. However, using the tips at the beginning of this book, you can also use visualization techniques or any other psychic abilities that you have developed. Visualization techniques used for this purpose involve inspecting the person's chakra system and finding blockages, conjuring an image of their aura, and much more. Here are some methods you can try:

Use a Photo

Ask your client to send you a photo of themselves, preferably a full body shot. This can serve you as a visual aid for your intuition. Look at the image and contours of their body and try to imagine their aura as a bright light enveloping them. Search for any dark spots which will be where energy is needed most. You can do the same with their chakras, except you need to look a little harder for specific clues that indicate an imbalance. Once you have established the source of the problem, you can use telepathy to send Reiki right to the body part where it is most needed. At the end of the session, visualize how the transferred energy envelops the problematic area.

Use a Surrogate

If you do not have a recipient's picture, you can also use a surrogate object to make a connection. This can be anything from a personal belonging, a doll that looks like them, to a random item that you can associate with the person. Set your intention while holding this object and visualize your energy enveloping it. You can combine this with the sandwich sequence or simply hold the distance healing symbol over the surrogate body just as you do with the name on the paper method. Using your psychic powers, try sensing where the energy is needed. See how the energy is transferred to the surrogate and on to the recipient. An added benefit of this method is that you can see which areas of their body need more attention. After a check-in with your intuition, you'll know where the root of the issue is. You can even visualize the object representing that particular part of the body and not necessarily the entire body. While you can not send physical energy directly to the affected area, you can make this an intent through the telepathic transfer. The recipient's mind will register it as their own intent and focus its energy on repairing the issue.

Using Other Symbols

Should you choose not to use the traditional Reiki Sandwich sequence, you can even leave out using symbols. You can choose to empower yourself with only one if you feel you only need a little assistance. You can also draw your own symbols, which can have multiple benefits. This helps sharpen your intuitive powers like any other technique involving listening to your gut does. Instead of drawing or visualizing a traditional symbol after focusing on your intent, you just draw or imagine whatever sign comes to mind first.

In fact, you can even do this without concentrating on the treatment you are trying to provide. Your mind is the most relaxed when it does not have to deal with the pressure of performing, and this is exactly the right time to tap into your intuition. Do something that relaxes you, and keep a pen and paper beside you. This way, you can free draw a symbol whenever it comes to you.

The other huge benefit of drawing individual symbols for treating others is that they allow you to create deeper connections. After scanning a person's body in real life, you become aware of any potential issues in their chakra system. This is not the case with distance healing, so connecting with a person's energy system and channeling your power into it is inherently more challenging. However, by getting to know them and using your intuition, you can find the right symbol to boost your ability to channel the vital life force through time and space. A symbol designed for a person's specific needs will always allow you to make stronger telepathic connections.

A person needing a vital life force is not the only entity you can form powerful telepathic connections using your intuition. If needed, you can also use your psychic abilities to request assistance from your spiritual guides or the Spirit of Reiki. Just as they can help you find the right course of treatment, so can they send a symbol to enhance your abilities.

Benefits of Distance Healing

Besides the obvious factor of enabling you to help anywhere, anytime, distance healing comes with plenty of other benefits for you and your client. When channeling energy with your psychic abilities, you raise positive vibrations that keep the negative ones at bay. The more powerful the energy bursts are, as they have to be for you to send them through space and time, and the more often they happen, the cleaner your environment will be.

Distance healing eliminates the need to cleanse your space before each client. Since you do not have to prepare your workspace for each client, you can have a larger client base. Consequently, you can help more people who need this precious life force. Many people don't have Reiki practitioners available in their area, and traveling to one would increase their discomfort. Through distance healing, everyone can get the relief they need.

Some people may not feel comfortable enough in your workspace to just sit or lay down, close their eyes, and relax their body and mind. However, if they can do this in the comfort of their homes, they will become much more relaxed and ready to embrace Reiki in no time.

At the end of the day, distance healing is a much safer and more effective method of distributing Reiki energy. With powerful positive emotions, you can send an enormous boost to someone's chakra system in just a few minutes. If someone needs quick assistance in an unexpected situation, you'll be able to help them out regardless of your location.

Disclaimer

Since distance can affect the efficiency of the treatment, there are fewer contraindications than for hand placement or any other treatment conducted close to your subject. And as vibrations are being transformed over an extended period, they will not have such a drastic effect on the person's body. Instead, the gradual changes have long-lasting benefits improving their lives and making them happier and healthier. That said, distance healing is still a much-debated alternative healing method, which is not recognized by medical professionals either. The same rules apply to other Reiki sessions. Any medical condition should be treated with conventional medicine, and the physical energy should only serve as an aid.

This assistance should not be provided during surgery, particularly if the person is undergoing general anesthesia. Being under anesthesia prevents the mind from regulating its functions. Any alterations to one's energy system during this period can cause issues during and after surgery. You need to be aware of this as you are honing your telepathic abilities. For example, if someone close to you is having surgery, you may intuitively want to send them Reiki energy to help them get through the procedure. Make sure to wait until they start their post-operative recovery process to send them healing energy.

Chapter 10: Activate Your Third Eye Temple

The journey to one's Third Eye Temple involves different techniques. The landscape within the Third Eye chakra can be used for various psychic purposes and is ideal for enhancing psychic healing. This chapter explains the measures you can take to activate your third eye temple. We also cover the following aspects:

- What you can do in this temple
- How can the temple be used?
- What can you ask your guides?
- How do you solve specific problems or heal blockages?

We will give you insight into the different purposes for which you can use your Third Eye area in Reiki and explain through detailed steps how to connect with Reiki through the Third Eye.

Understanding the Third Eye Temple

Also known as the sixth chakra or sixth sense in the body, and situated in the center of your forehead, parallel to your eyebrows, it is believed to be connected to awareness, perception, and spiritual communication.

When this chakra is utilized, great insight and wisdom can be found. It also deepens your spiritual connection, which is extremely useful for healing.

The third eye chakra relates to traits like concentration, clarity, intuition, imagination, universal connection, and spiritual perception. It is believed to be connected to the cone-shaped, pea-sized pineal gland. It is viewed as a critical tool by mystics and seers and is believed to provide a universal connection. Most cultures recognize the pineal gland as being biologically linked to the third eye chakra.

What Can the Third Eye Chakra Do?

The chakra is viewed as the gateway to the spiritual world, including all psychic things. It also helps you get clear vision, removes mental blockages, and improves your mental flexibility. Many cultures see it as the most important sense – *and activating it is critical.*

If your third eye chakra is blocked, you'll probably feel fatigued, stuck, have low creativity, be pessimistic, fear success, lack motivation, and will repress memories. You may also face different problems – including confusion and uncertainty. The third eye sees the true world and its spiritual connections, whereas our eyes see the physical aspects. If you experience any of these signs, it means that your third eye must be activated. There are many advantages to activating your Third eye temple. When your third eye is opened, your mind becomes calmer and more focused. Whatever you do in life for a living, you are likely to experience a positive change following the activation of the third eye. The following are some of the experiences that come with opening your third eye chakra.

- **Wisdom:** Third eye activation gives you wisdom, enlightening you so that you can separate the truth from illusion. In other words, it gives you the wisdom of enlightenment.
- **Better Attention:** Your attention to detail significantly improves if your third eye is open. Your mind becomes more focused, and you'll have a heightened awareness of things that happen around you. Your senses of hearing, sight, and taste become sharper.
- **Enjoy Peace:** When your third eye chakra is activated, you can enjoy more peace, and anger issues will subside. You

will find that irritation and anger will no longer affect you when the eye is open, and you'll feel at peace. Third eye activation also leads to a deep sense of calmness in your mind.

- **Devotion:** Third eye activation leads to devotion, which is an experience of the heart. Mental clarity leads to focus and improved concentration. It gives you insight and decisiveness when dealing with different issues.

How the Third Eye Affects Our Mental Health

The third eye chakra can affect us emotionally and spiritually in many ways, although mainstream science does not support the link. Yet, there have been many anecdotal reports of unexplained happenings connected to the third eye. It can often be used as a gateway to the spirit world. The following are some of the effects of telepathy on our minds.

Telepathy

Telepathy involves direct communication between two minds and is not just a myth. The mind can perceive someone else's thoughts without using recognized senses. This is known as telepathic communication, where the mind transmits information to another mind. When another person's beliefs or thoughts influence someone's mind, it is known as mind control.

Mind control can be influenced by the third eye temple, where influence comes from outside. However, it can also lead to destruction, and this is usually determined by the person imposing their power on someone's mind. The kind of knowledge passed through telepathic communication offers benefits and disadvantages, so you must believe your instincts.

Clairvoyance

Clairvoyance helps you predict the future, which can be influenced by your third eye when activated. The energy center also helps you do more than predict the future. You will be aware of the big picture when you open your third eye. The ability to see everything helps shift your perspective, so you can have a clear view of your blind spots and understand everything from the collective perspective. However, to use your third eye to see through space and time, you must first use it to see yourself.

Lucid Dreaming

Lucid dreaming happens when you are conscious, and many people have experienced this in their lifetime. It is a form of metacognition or awareness of your consciousness. During a lucid dream, you control what happens, which is only possible if your third eye chakra is open. In some cases, dreams come true, and they can give you guidance in your life. If you activate your third eye, you can interpret dreams.

How to Open Your Third Eye

The rituals to open your third eye should not be complicated since they include simple steps. The following are some methods you can consider opening the third eye.

Touch

You can use touch to awaken the energy in your third eye temple. You can use your finger to press or tap the third eye, and you need to recite your favorite affirmation while touching the temple. This is a simple ritual you can do anywhere, and it does not require special tools or equipment to perform.

Visualization

Visualization is another technique that you can consider for awakening your third eye. This process requires focus, so anything that can improve your attention will help open it. The method of visualization involves the following three steps.

- Hold any object in front of your eyes and try to study its details. Take your time to record your observations in your mind.

- Close your eyes and try to visualize the object you have been holding. Take about 30 minutes trying to concentrate on the item you studied.

- Repeat the process every day. You can also extend your concentration time and practice with more complex objects.

This exercise helps ground your vision so you can handle the insights that require higher consciousness.

Activate the Third Eye Chakra

To activate your third eye, begin by sending gratitude to it. This will stimulate your intuitive abilities and connection to nature. Your pineal gland regulates your sleep-wake cycle, which is important for properly opening your third eye.

Supplement Your Diet

If you eat well, you can do much more, including opening your third eye. There are many foods you can include in your diet that will support your third eye – and some that will limit you. Eat lots of nuts, berries, garlic, seeds, coconut, honey, herbs, and foods with vitamin D3. These all help with your pineal gland, which, in turn, supports the third eye.

Apply Essential Oils

Essential oils can heal ailments.
https://pixabay.com/images/id-3532970/

Essential oils can heal many ailments and boost your health – and they can also work wonders for opening your third eye. You can create your own essential oil blends, and most essential oils will be beneficial, but jasmine and sandalwood are recommended. Always use a carrier oil to dilute the essential oils to make sure the blend is safe.

When mixing in a carrier oil, you don't need much essential oil, and 5-7 drops will suffice. Because your third eye is between the eyes, dab a little on your forehead to open your third eye.

Remember to use your chant as you apply the oil and once it is applied.

Sun Gazing

You can harness the power of the sun to awaken your third eye. Never look directly at the sun when it is in the sky, but gaze close to it at sunrise and sunset. Spend a few minutes each time, and you can also meditate as you do this to better awaken the third eye. The sun's power affects your pineal gland, activating the third eye.

Meditate and Chant

Meditation plays a pivotal role in activating the pineal gland through intention and vibration. It helps channel our energies, improve concentration, and remove negative toxins from the body. The third eye connects us to our gut feelings and works ahead of our five senses. However, to enjoy the benefits of the sixth sense, you must open your dormant eye. This is where meditation comes in handy and is viewed as the best way to awaken and activate your third eye.

There are different forms of meditation you can consider, and these are designed to help you improve your awareness and shift your consciousness to a higher level. This will help you remove anxiety and other forms of worry. Meditation also helps your mind work to the fullest and improves concentration.

Like any form of meditation, you must stay calm in a quiet environment and listen to the soothing sounds of music. Try to find a perfect place to sit comfortably on the chair or floor. You should relax your shoulders, keep your spine erect, and your hands on your knees. Other parts of your body like the stomach, face, and jaw must be relaxed, and make sure that your body is open to positive energy.

You can begin by bringing your index finger to the thumb and gently closing your eyes. Breathe slowly, and make sure you use your nose to inhale and exhale with your eyes still closed. Try to look at the third eye between your eyebrows; you can also use your fingers to locate it. While breathing slowly, try to channel your gaze at this point and concentrate on it for some minutes. Continue doing this until you see bluish-white or white light beginning to appear. When you reach this stage, you enter a stage of healing, and your concentration will be at the highest level and most effective. You want to let go of bad energies at this stage, and focus should be your top priority.

Chant as you meditate to help the bone in your nose to resonate. This will stimulate the pineal gland that is linked to your third eye. Chanting also helps you to focus on the things you are grateful for in your life. When you meditate, it is vital to appreciate the significance of the third eye. What you chant should come from your heart, and make sure that you include the things you want to achieve once your third eye chakra is activated.

Meditation is a simple exercise since there is no strict rule to follow. Stay in your meditation position for a few seconds, then blink your eyes. You can continue with your regular activities when you are finished. You can meditate every morning or a few minutes before going to bed. This will work wonders in healing and activating your chakras. Just make sure that you are focused on what you want to achieve regarding your third eye chakra.

Use Crystals

Crystals have healing energies and are believed to be crucial in opening your third eye. Choose purple colors of gemstones to boost your third eye. Purple, and similar colors, are excellent for creating balance, opening the third eye, and signing the self.

Place the crystals of gemstones between your eyes on top of your third eye. Gemstones are believed to possess the energy that can stimulate your chakras. Different stones are used for various purposes, so you must choose the ones that suit your needs.

How Long Does Your Third Eye Chakra Take to Open?

That depends on the person. It will change from person to person and will also change during the year and even by the time of day. And, even if you do open your third eye, it is considered a lifelong practice that you never truly master—only improve on. You can dedicate as much time as you like each day to opening your third eye, and fifteen minutes every day should be sufficient using the above practices. Don't force it; wait for the eye to open naturally – as if you are waking from sleep.

How Do You Know If Your Third Eye Is Open?

Your third eye chakra is your sixth sense, and that is going to help guide you intuitively through life, so if you feel your sixth sense is helping you, then your chakra is likely to open. Use your intuition to develop your third eye once it is open. Your sixth sense is also linked to wisdom, growth, healing, and the spirit. Meditate even if you think your eye is open, and continue to practice each day while maintaining your health.

Chapter 11: The Psychic Reiki Toolkit: Crystals, Talismans, Trinkets, and Tarot

Everything in life is connected by energy, and Reiki healing makes the most of this energy field. This chapter will discuss the tools you'll need in your healing kit, from crystal to tarot and everything in between. And we discuss how you can use each one and the expected outcome they can bring to your healing practice.

Crystals and Gemstones

Crystals are conduits for the earth's healing energy.
https://www.pexels.com/photo/photo-of-assorted-crsytals-4040639/

When used properly, crystals are conduits for the earth's healing energy. They emit uplifting, positive, calming, and energizing vibrations that help your mind to be revitalized and peaceful. There are different types of crystals or gemstones, and each piece has a specific use on the body and mind. The vibrations and energies produced by crystals have healing powers, and they affect us in various ways. However, medical experts say no scientific research supports the efficacy of crystals in healing diseases.

Although there are mixed reactions to the healing powers of crystals, these stones have some form of physical and mental benefits, which can be attributed to the placebo effect. Many people have great faith in the healing power of prayer, and the same applies to crystals. The placebo effect is supported by scientific research, and the other thing is that crystals do not cause any harm to your health. Adding gems to your life can increase your confidence and positive energy.

When choosing gemstones, you must determine your wellness needs because different crystals are used for different ailments. These precious stones come in different colors and can be used as jewelry. Some give you a sense of calm when you carry them with you, and different crystals are good for helping you to meditate. The following are the types of crystals you can include in your toolkit.

- Clear quartz is ideal for beginners since it provides more energy and also charges your intentions when meditating.
- Black Tourmaline has protective properties and will guard you against negative energy. To protect your environment, place this stone on your desk, at your front door, or in the corners of your room to secure the environment.
- Amethysts offer calming energy and help you relax at night. You can put this stone under your pillow for a peaceful sleep. This crystal is good for you, particularly after a hectic day.
- Citrine represents light, joy, and happiness. If you are feeling low, you can invoke the powers of this stone.
- Aquamarine can be worn as a necklace and helps you speak the truth. This type of stone is a good accessory if you have speech deficiency. The stone also helps you

achieve your goals when undertaking creative projects.
- Rose Quartz is associated with love and helps open your heart. You can keep it in your bedroom for consistent results.
- Tiger's Eye is a grounding stone that helps improve your physical performance in different activities like sports.
- Moonstone helps your heart when you are feeling low.
- Pink opal helps you release anger and tension.
- Kyanite is good for daily life and bolsters the mind and body link.

Regardless of what crystal you choose, make sure that you charge it by leaving it to sit outside in direct moonlight or sunlight for about four hours. Sunlight and moonlight are crucial as they help your crystal hold more energy. A charged crystal can support you in a way you may not see, but you'll feel the impact.

You must set clear intentions and visualize how you'll achieve your goals. You can achieve this by holding the stones in your hands and sitting quietly. Start thinking about your goals; the stone will absorb your intention and activate. Once it is charged, you can use it any way you like. For instance, you can wear it as a necklace, keep it in your office, or simply hold it whenever you want to revive your intention. Healing stones can be used together with other practices such as meditation.

Scrying Spheres and Bowls

The process of gazing into a bowl or crystal ball is known as scrying, and it is mainly used to divine the unknown. The goal of scrying is to help you receive or see messages, pictures, scenes, or symbols that possess information not previously known. There are different types of tools that can be used, like scrying spheres, bowls, or crystal balls. You can also consider cloud and water scrying.

When you look into the surface of your chosen item, your third eye will begin to separate from your body, and you'll feel as if you are meditating. You will see darkness in your vision; half of it should be black. When you reach this state, you'll begin to hear voices or see messages, pictures, and symbols. If you want to scry in a bowl or crystal ball, you need to follow the steps below.

- Take out the ball from its storage to set up the stage.
- Cleanse the ball using your favorite, most effective way.
- Create a sacred space where you can put your crystal ball at a comfortable height so you can easily gaze into it. Light a few candles, use sage to cleanse the space, light your favorite incense and turn on your favorite music.
- Turn on a voice recording app, so you do not miss crucial details that you might miss if you are just trying to write everything down.
- Sit comfortably as this process can take a long time.
- Begin gazing and count backward from 12, and try to visualize each number in the ball.
- When you are done with your countdown, take some time to look into the center of the ball, and you'll begin to see dark spots, black blobs, or clouds. This marks the beginning of your vision, and you must ensure that you lock your vision on the dark clouds once you see them.
- Ask questions when you begin to hear something from the clouds. Say everything you hear aloud so you can record it.
- End your session by counting from 1 to 12, and thank the spirits for guiding you.
- Cleanse the tools and put them back in their storage.

You should practice scrying often because it helps you fall into a trance quickly. Remember to choose an appropriate tool for your session. You can practice this healing method whenever you need answers to something you feel is impacting your life.

Tarot/Oracle Cards

Tarot and oracle cards can also be used for different purposes in Reiki. The readings are mainly used for clairvoyant sessions where the reader interprets messages conveyed by the tarot cards. You can ask anything you want; the readings are usually conducted in about 30 minutes. The cards will focus on all the different things you want to know.

If you want to know something about your career, you can ask the tarot cards, and you'll get your answer from an interpreter. You can also learn to interpret the messages, but this can take time. In any session, you can use direct questioning, and the reader will be able to give you answers related to your finances, work, and other areas that can affect your life.

Talismans and Sacred Items

Talismans and other sacred items are symbols of protection and can be used in various situations. For instance, you can use a protective talisman to protect your space, as well as protect memories from unwanted disruption or negative energy. Talismans can be worn, or you can keep them in appropriate places where they can protect.

The Reiki source energy can also be infused into crystals, which magnifies their healing power. A talisman or bracelet consists of various healing crystals that magnify the purpose of intent when infused. One thing about crystals is that they consist of different charms and energy that can solve various issues in life.

Reiki-infused jewelry is also used to provide support or boost your intentions. You can also get a talisman when you need a dose of love. If you are busy with other commitments, an amulet will provide quick healing or a solution to your problem. You can wear your charged bracelet the way you want, providing healing powers. Others wear bracelets to keep evil spirits at bay.

Trinkets

Like talismans, different types of trinkets can be used in Reiki sessions. Common trinkets include jewelry, heirlooms, figurines, and anything meaningful to the practitioner. These items can also be used to send telepathic healing messages. Your trinket can give you the power to communicate with other people or simply receive messages.

You can also get a bracelet that holds healing powers or is capable of keeping you calm. These bracelets are made from different materials and come in different shapes and sizes. Before you buy a bracelet, you should spell your intention and outline the goals you want to achieve. Understanding the purpose of each material used in the bracelet is vital. You can also use the Reiki charged bracelet in healing sessions and must state your intention.

Reiki Water

Wondering how you can charge water with Reiki? You can use your charged water for drinking, watering plants, or for any other healing work. Making Reiki water is simple as the entire process only requires your intention. Churches use prayers to charge their water while blessings of the spirit are invoked in sacred locations.

If you get in touch with undisturbed nature, it consists of some sacredness similar to that experienced by religious people. While there is no scientific explanation of how water is charged, it is strongly believed that different methods can be used. Charged water can be used specifically for energy healing. The other critical issue is that energy flows around us and not only inside, so when we interact with the environment or other people, energy flow is touched by that interaction.

Our state of health is determined by how freely the energy in our bodies can circulate and flow. While energy therapists are trained to detect the energy flows through their hands and create optimal conditions, hydrotherapy is a perfect method that can be used to ensure optimum energy flow.

This therapy can take place in a hydrotherapy pool consisting of charged water. You get into the pool to relax and enjoy an environment, and energy is at its optimum power while you are relaxing. However, you can feel some form of temporary discomfort in specific parts of the body while they are realigning. After the session in the hydrotherapy pool, you'll feel energized and refreshed. Water heals, and you can immediately feel its benefits once you move out of the pool.

You can also drink Reiki water, and it will provide healing powers. This water is used after a treatment session. You will often feel thirsty after the treatment. Many people feel the difference in their bodies during and after the treatment, which rebalances the energy system in your body. If you take a bath using charged water, you'll feel rejuvenated and energized.

If you are a novice in the world of Reiki healing, these are different tools you should know about. The items explained in this chapter can be used for various healing, so you should know your intention first. Make sure that all tools are charged or energized for the best results. When you use any tool for healing, make your intention known and always repeat it.

Conclusion

Reiki energy provides a unique healing power. Once you master this technique, you can help people through gentle touch. In this book, we have provided you with all the information you need to use your psychic power and start your journey as a psychic Reiki practitioner. We began this book by explaining the concept of Reiki, its principles, and its symbols. As a beginner, to give you the full experience, we made sure to include what takes place during a Reiki session.

To become a psychic Reiki practitioner, there are certain things to familiarize yourself with, such as energies, chakras, meditation, and visualization. We have dedicated two chapters in this book to provide you with everything you need to know about these four concepts. We have also included exercises and techniques so you can apply everything you have learned to yourself.

Having psychic abilities is a valuable gift. However, if you do not work on nurturing these abilities, you'll feel stuck and will lack the creativity to help others. Spiritual guides, clearing, and grounding can help improve your gift to be a better healer. We have also introduced the concept of the "Clairs" and how they can develop your psychic abilities, so you can expand on your intuition.

The second part of the book is mainly focused on healing. You can not heal others before first healing yourself. For this reason, we have included exercises to help you perform self-healing techniques. This is a vital skill every beginner should master before they start working with patients. We have provided a detailed explanation of how to connect with Reiki and draw from its energy. After healing yourself, you'll be ready to heal others. You will combine your psychic gift and your knowledge of Reiki to help them feel better.

We have also discussed using both telepathic and psychic abilities, so you can perform "distance healing" using various healing symbols and techniques. Psychics should have more than their regular eyes open. They should activate their third eye as well and journey into its temple. We have dedicated a whole chapter to activating the third eye temple and answering all the related questions, including how to activate your third eye chakra.

We ended the book by discussing all the tools a practitioner will need in their practice, like crystals, tarots, trinkets, and Reiki water. To help get you started, we have offered tips on how to use these tools and how to incorporate them into Reiki sessions.

By now, you have become familiar with the psychic Reiki topic. Use everything you have learned so far to heal others and yourself. Whenever you have a question or feel stuck with something, come back to this book, and you'll find an answer.

Here's another book by Mari Silva that you might like

Your Free Gift (only available for a limited time)

Thanks for getting this book! If you want to learn more about various spirituality topics, then join Mari Silva's community and get a free guided meditation MP3 for awakening your third eye. This guided meditation mp3 is designed to open and strengthen ones third eye so you can experience a higher state of consciousness. Simply visit the link below the image to get started.

https://spiritualityspot.com/meditation

References

Sacks, B., & Religion News Service. (2014, May 16). Reiki goes mainstream: Spiritual touch practice now commonplace in hospitals. Washington Post (Washington, D.C.: 1974). https://www.washingtonpost.com/national/religion/reiki-goes-mainstream-spiritual-touch-practice-now-commonplace-in-hospitals/2014/05/16/9e92223a-dd37-11e3-a837-8835df6c12c4_story.html

Types of complementary and alternative medicine. (2019, November 19). Hopkinsmedicine.Org. https://www.hopkinsmedicine.org/health/wellness-and-prevention/types-of-complementary-and-alternative-medicine

Adam, B. (2018, November 5). What is a Reiki attunement? My Blog. https://www.pathwayshealing.com/what-is-a-reiki-attunement/

Administrator, R. (2014, October 15). What is Reiki? Reiki. https://www.reiki.org/faqs/what-reiki

Bedosky, L., & Laube, J. (n.d.). Reiki: How this energy healing works and its health benefits. EverydayHealth.Com. https://www.everydayhealth.com/reiki/

Cauldrons, & Cupcakes. (2019, January 22). Are You A Sensitive, Intuitive, Psychic, or Empathic Soul? Here's a Checklist to help you find out! Cauldrons and Cupcakes. https://cauldronsandcupcakes.com/2019/01/23/are-you-a-sensitive-intuitive-psychic-or-empathic-soul-heres-a-checklist-to-help-you-find-out/

Cronkleton, E. (2018, June 21). Reiki: Benefits, what to expect, crystals, finding a practitioner. Healthline. https://www.healthline.com/health/reiki

Daly, A. (2019, April 22). Reiki might actually be worth A try if you're in pain. Women's Health. https://www.womenshealthmag.com/health/a27155104/what-is-reiki/

Everything you need to know about reiki symbols & their meanings. (2018, May 8). Mindbodygreen. https://www.mindbodygreen.com/articles/reiki-symbols-meanings/

How does Reiki work? (n.d.). Taking Charge of Your Health & Wellbeing. https://www.takingcharge.csh.umn.edu/explore-healing-practices/reiki/how-does-reiki-work

IARP. (2014, April 20). History of Reiki: Read about the origin and traditions of Reiki. IARP. https://iarp.org/history-of-reiki/

Luna, A. (2016, June 6). 30 signs you're born to be a spiritual healer. LonerWolf. https://lonerwolf.com/spiritual-healer/

Marcovigil, Giselle, Sam, Brown, S., Robert, Lisa, & K. (2020, June 26). How to tell if you are psychic? 6 signs you are A psychic medium. The Black Feather Intuitive. https://www.theblackfeatherintuitive.com/how-to-tell-if-you-are-psychic/

Naicker, X. (2021, September 6). 7 signs you're a healer and not just sensitive (updated in 2022). Mysticmag.Com; MysticMag. https://www.mysticmag.com/psychic-reading/signs-you-might-be-a-healer/

Nunez, K. (2020, August 24). Reiki principles and how to use them to boost well-being. Healthline. https://www.healthline.com/health/reiki-principles

Reiki Attunement - the process and the purpose. (2018, January 8). Centre of Excellence. https://www.centreofexcellence.com/reiki-attunement-process-purpose/

Rohan, E. (2022, May 20). Today's menopause solutions Aren't your mom's hot-flash remedies (I know because I asked mine). Well+Good. https://www.wellandgood.com/menopause-solutions-phenology/

Star, D. B. (2015). What Is Reiki? Createspace Independent Publishing Platform.

What is Reiki, and Does it Really Work? (2021, August 30). Cleveland Clinic. https://health.clevelandclinic.org/reiki/

(N.d.-a). Yourlegacyproject.Com. https://yourlegacyproject.com/10-signs-you-are-a-healer/

(N.d.-b). Com.Au. https://www.bodyandsoul.com.au/mind-body/10-surprising-signs-that-you-might-be-psychic/news-story/7220ada2fd93f329915bbaa529a78eb6

Biernacki, L. (2019). Subtle body. In Transformational Embodiment in Asian Religions (pp. 108–127). Routledge.

Davis, F. (2021, March 3). 11 ways to enhance your life force energy: Tap into the best version of you. Cosmic Cuts. https://cosmiccuts.com/blogs/healing-stones-blog/life-force-energy

Evolution Yoga. (2019, August 27). Chanting the chakra sounds and the nervous system. Evolution Physical Therapy and Yoga. https://evolutionvt.com/chanting-the-chakra/

Flinn, A. (2021, July 19). Your guide to auras: What they are & what to expect during A reading. Mindbodygreen. https://www.mindbodygreen.com/0-25407/what-is-an-aura-and-how-can-you-see-yours.html

Holland, K. (2022, January 5). What is an aura? 16 FAQs about seeing auras, colors, layers, and more. Healthline. https://www.healthline.com/health/what-is-an-aura

How to make an energy ball of chi. (2011, April 28). LEAFtv. https://www.leaf.tv/articles/how-to-make-an-energy-ball-of-chi/

Jain, R. (2019, June 13). Complete guide to 7 chakras & their effects. Arhanta Yoga Ashrams. https://www.arhantayoga.org/blog/7-chakras-introduction-energy-centers-effect/

Jain, R. (2020a, August 24). Muladhara Chakra, Root Chakra - complete guide. Arhanta Yoga Ashrams. https://www.arhantayoga.org/blog/all-you-need-to-know-about-muladhara-chakra-root-chakra/

Jain, R. (2020b, August 26). Svadhishthana - Sacral Chakra: All you need to know. Arhanta Yoga Ashrams. https://www.arhantayoga.org/blog/svadhishthana-chakra-all-you-need-to-know-about-the-sacral-chakra/

Jain, R. (2020c, September 3). Manipura Chakra: Healing powers of Solar Plexus Chakra. Arhanta Yoga Ashrams. https://www.arhantayoga.org/blog/manipura-chakra-healing-powers-of-the-solar-plexus-chakra/

Jain, R. (2020d, September 16). Anahata Chakra - Heart Chakra: Self-realization through love. Arhanta Yoga Ashrams. https://www.arhantayoga.org/blog/anahata-chakra-heart-chakra-self-realization-through-love/

Jain, R. (2020e, September 22). Vishuddha Chakra: How to balance your Throat Chakra. Arhanta Yoga Ashrams. https://www.arhantayoga.org/blog/vishuddha-chakra-balance-how-to-balance-your-throat-chakra/

Jain, R. (2020f, October 8). Crown chakra: The divine energy of Sahasrara chakra. Arhanta Yoga Ashrams. https://www.arhantayoga.org/blog/crown-chakra-divine-energy-of-sahasrara-chakra/

Lindberg, S. (2020, August 24). What are chakras? Meaning, location, and how to unblock them. Healthline. https://www.healthline.com/health/what-are-chakras

Printed in Great Britain
by Amazon